NATIVE PEOPLES

of the

Olympic Peninsula

Crossing the Shoulder of de Fuca
PAUL KN...

NATIVE PEOPLES
of the
Olympic Peninsula

—— WHO WE ARE ——

by the Olympic Peninsula Intertribal
Cultural Advisory Committee

Edited by Jacilee Wray

Publication of this book is made possible through the generosity of Edith Kinney Gaylord.

ON THE TITLE PAGE: The indigenous people of the Olympic Peninsula frequently traveled by canoe across the Strait of Juan de Fuca to Vancouver Island. Canadian artist Paul Kane depicted his May 1847 canoe journey across the strait in his painting *Crossing the Strait of Juan de Fuca*, which is on this book's frontispiece and title page (Courtesy of the Stark Museum of Art, Orange, Texas).

Library of Congress Cataloging-in-Publication Data

Native peoples of the Olympic Peninsula : who we are / by the Olympic Peninusla
    Intertribal Cultural Advisory Committee ; edited by Jacilee Wray.
       p. cm.
    Includes bibliographical references and index.
    ISBN 0–8061–3394–5 (hardcover : alk. paper)
    1. Indians of North America—Washington (State)—Olympic Peninsula. I. Wray,
       Jacilee. II. Olympic Peninsula Intertribal Cultural Advisory Committee.
E78.W3 N37 2002
305.897'079794—dc21   2001040613

We dedicate this book to the future of our ideas, the tribal youth.

Wesley Whitener and Annie Krise Whitener.
Courtesy of Whitener Family.

Our old ways are mostly memories, but our ideas march to their beat.

—Squaxin Island tribal elders

Contents

Illustrations

Figures

Maps

Foreword

The indigenous peoples of the Olympic Peninsula share a rich history. For centuries, however, their stories have not been available to the general public. This important volume breaks new ground by letting us read their stories in their own words. It puts a collection of oral traditions into written form, opening a new window onto the life, spirit, and experiences of some of our region's earliest inhabitants.

As I have traveled our state and spoken with members of the various Olympic tribes, I have been moved by the people and their stories. This book shares the rich legacy of the Olympic Peninsula tribes with all of us—offering a living testament to these ancient and vibrant nations. It puts their distinctive stories in the hands of students, historians, visitors, and everyone interested in the region's history.

Of course, no historical account of indigenous peoples would be complete without stories of broken treaties and unkept promises. I hope this book will improve our understanding of these tribes and our shared history. By shining light on our past, this book can help us to build a future together based on mutual respect and understanding.

I am pleased this volume adds a new and unique voice to the chorus of our region's history. One of the great traditions of these cultures is the belief in their responsibility to pass down stories from one generation to the next. This book expands that tradition, and I am proud to support this important and inspiring effort.

Patty Murray
United States Senator

Preface

In June 1992 representatives of Indian tribes of the Olympic Peninsula and contiguous areas formed the Olympic Peninsula Intertribal Cultural Advisory Committee (OPICAC). The committee meets at one of our nine reservations every other month to work toward carrying out our mission:

> The OPICAC represents a concerted effort to address salient cultural issues through traditionally based responses. Our mission is to act as a cultural advisory committee that represents our traditional values as coastal tribes with acknowledgment and respect for our unique tribal differences. We are committed to the understanding, preservation, and continuation of cultural knowledge in all regards: origins, histories, and stories; land areas and waterways and their uses; traditions, values, and beliefs; language, song, and dance; mental, physical, and spiritual well-being; the cultural uses of animal life, marine life, and plant life; and all other aspects of tribal identity.

The goals of the committee include educating those who do not have a clear understanding of who we are. All too often non-Indians have a romantic view of us. At cultural celebrations, thousands of photographs are taken of dancers in full regalia, but how many see the elders, the children, the mothers, and fathers there? As one elder pointed out, "I don't need to wear beads to prove I am an Indian. I know who I am."

A tribe not only consists of individuals in traditional roles; a storyteller, basket weaver, or fisherman may also be a mill worker, a lawyer, a teacher, or a government representative. Tribal members may live on or off the reservation; they help their children with homework and teach traditional knowledge, they pull canoes and handle motorized boats, and they speak English yet strive to preserve their native language. We have changed, but more important, we have held onto or revived the traditions that make us unique, strong, and healthy in our culture and communities.

American Indians represent from 12 to 97 percent of the student bodies in the peninsula school districts, yet many of the school curricula do not teach the history and the contemporary issues that affect tribes today. Often schools teach about a generalized Northwest culture. It is true that Olympic Peninsula tribes are categorized within the Pacific Coast culture because of general lifestyle elements we share with our neighbors to the north and south: fishing, land and marine hunting, traditional ceremonies, cedar carving, and canoe travel. However, our relationship with the peninsula landscape is unique and distinctive. This relationship spans tens of thousands of years and is based on beliefs and practices tied to specific areas and experiences. Each of the nine tribes represented in this book shares a similar history. Each signed treaties between 1854 and 1856 and ceded traditional lands for small reservations. Soon after we were "supervised" on our reservations by missionaries, schoolteachers, and Indian agents who set restrictions on passing on our languages and traditions to our children. All of us have sought to protect our right to fish, hunt, and gather, and after years of struggle we are succeeding. The peninsula tribes continue to share the strength, courage, and humor that have enabled us to preserve our heritage for future generations.

In 1996 the OPICAC decided that the best way to increase understanding of our heritage would be to produce a publication that would provide a foundation for learning about the people who are a part of the history and community here and now. The committee received a grant from the National Park Foundation to support our work on this project, as well as a contribution from the National Park Service Challenge Cost Share program. We also received college credit in writing and editing from the Northwest Indian College. We had previously received a grant from the National Park Service Historic Preservation Fund to assist with travel to meetings and to provide training in historic preservation.

The efforts of the committee representatives, who were delegated by their tribes, resulted in this volume. In addition to the lead authors, tribal cultural specialists assisted with writing, finding photographs, and conducting research; our elders provided guidance and insight; and tribal councils reviewed the chapters. The many people who have come together to see this book come to fruition are committed to the enlightenment of generations to come.

The tribes of the peninsula region share complex histories of trade, religion, warfare, and kinship, as well as reverence for the teachings of our elders. We are neighbors who travel for miles to attend intertribal meetings. Some of us also come together for weddings, naming ceremonies, and other cultural events or to share the practice of traditional skills, a continuation of social interchange among our tribes.

We have withstood the loss of our lands and have adapted to changing circumstances. Some change is good; for example, we choose motorized skiffs over dugout canoes when we travel our ancient rivers. Although the technology is different, our skill and knowledge of the rivers has not diminished. The difference between early adaptations and those that have taken place over the past centuries is that before the treaties to cede our lands, we had more freedom to decide for ourselves which elements of our cultures we wished to save and which should change.

Tribal sovereignty, or self-determination, enables the tribes and their members to decide which features of their tribal culture and other cultures can coexist and which ones must be recast and adapted. As Anne Pavel of the Skokomish Tribe has stated, "We are not stupid, we know a good thing when we see it. If we had a bucket available, we would not continue to carry water in a basket."

The resurgence of canoe travel, celebrated with an annual intertribal canoe journey, teaches our communities valuable skills, not only canoe making and pulling, but also strength, cooperation, companionship, and perseverance. The journeys are an opportunity to reclaim long-held traditions such as the potlatch ceremony, singing, oration in our native languages, and dancing. They also provide a time to rekindle relationships with our relatives, our spirituality, and the forces of nature. During these long journeys, we become one with the surge of the tides, the elements, and all of nature's powers.

We are thankful every day for the teachings received from our past elders. They taught us many things. We did not always know what to ask, but they knew what to teach us. Now we need to teach others.

Acknowledgments

This book is the result of the collaborative efforts of the Olympic Peninsula Intertribal Cultural Advisory Committee: Marie Hebert (Port Gamble S'Klallam), Anne Pavel and Bonnie (James) Graft (Skokomish) Chris Morganroth III (Quileute), Kathy Duncan (Jamestown S'Klallam), Janine Bowechop and Melissa Peterson (Makah), Justine James and Leilani A. Chubby (Quinault), Viola Riebe (Hoh), Jamie Valadez and Georgianne Charles (Elwha Klallam), and Charlene Krise and Andi VanderWal (Squaxin Island).

The committee would like to thank Kate Reavey for her editing skills and support. The anthropologists Karen James and Jay Powell provided us with much of their time and expertise, and we are grateful for their assistance and friendship. Many individuals assisted the authors, and we would like to thank them: Shane Bowechop, Carol Brown, Beatrice Charles, Ed Claplanhoo, Rhonda Foster, Helen Harrison, Meredith P. Heilman, Keith Johnson, Kristan Kincade, Nancy LaClair, Kristina Laubner, Barbara Lawrence, Emily Mansfield, Bruce Miller, Maria Pascua, Phil Renault, Genny Rogers, Margaret Seymour-Henry, Mary Higgins Shaffer, Jill Silver, Adeline Smith, Yvonne Wilkie, and Liz Yeahquo. We would also like to thank Dave Conca, Richard Daugherty, Paul Gleeson, Tim Montler, Aaron Scrol, Brian Winter, and Fred York for sharing their expertise.

The National Park Service (NPS) Challenge Cost Share Program, the National Park Foundation, and the Northwest Indian College realized the importance of this project and assisted with funding.

We thank the management staff at Olympic National Park, the NPS Tribal Historic Preservation Fund Grant Program, the NPS Archeology and Ethnography Program, and the NPS American Indian Liaison Office for their support and encouragement of the intertribal committee.

Chronology

1700	Earthquake in Pacific Northwest causes tsunami in Japan
1775	Spanish Hezeta-Francisco de la Bodega y Quadra Expedition at Quinault
1787	Charles Barkley names Strait of Juan de Fuca and Destruction Island
1790	Spanish explorer Manuel Quimper lands at Freshwater Bay and Dungeness
1791	Port Angeles named Nuestra Señora de Los Angeles by Juan Francisco de Eliza
1792	Captain George Vancouver explores coastline of Olympic Peninsula
1808	Russian schooner *Sv. Nikolai* runs aground near La Push
1819	Spain surrenders claim to Northwest
1824	Russia surrenders claim to Northwest
1846	Establishment of 49th parallel/Oregon Territory
1847	Paul Kane crosses Strait of Juan de Fuca
1850	Donation Land Act of Oregon
1853	Washington Territory established
1854	Treaty of Medicine Creek
1855	Treaty of Neah Bay and Treaty of Point No Point
1855	March 3, Medicine Creek Treaty ratified
1855–56	Quinault River Treaty, or Treaty of Olympia
1856–57	Indian War, Puget Sound Indians fought for suitable land base
1859	March 8, Congress ratifies Olympic Peninsula treaties
1871	End of U.S./tribal treaty making
1875	Amendment of 1860 Homestead Act to extend to Indians
1880	Establishment of Chemawa boarding school in Oregon
1882	Origin of Shaker Religion
1884	Indian Homestead Act
1887	General Allotment Act
1889	Washington becomes forty-second state
1890	Press Expedition reaches Quinault River
1897	Olympic Forest Reserve proclaimed
1905	Construction of New Puget Sound Agency School (Tulalip Reservation)
1906	Burke Act, twenty-five year trust status on allotted lands may be removed
1910	Construction of first Elwha River dam begins
1924	Native Americans become U.S. citizens
1925	Construction of first Skokomish River dam begins
1934	Indian Reorganization Act
1934	Johnson-O'Malley Act
1938	Olympic National Park established
1946	Indian Claims Commission established
1953	Coastal Strip added to Olympic National Park

1966   National Historic Preservation Act (as amended)

1970   Ozette archaeological project begins (ends in 1981)

1974   *U.S. v. Washington* (Judge Boldt upholds tribal right to anadromous fish)

1975   Indian Self-Determination and Education Assistance Act

1977   Manis Mastodon Site discovered

1978   American Indian Religious Freedom Act

1988   Indian Gaming Regulatory Act to provide for tribal gaming

1989   Centennial Accord between Washington State and tribes

1990   Native American Graves Protection and Repatriation Act

1992   Olympic Peninsula Intertribal Cultural Advisory Committee established

1993   Governor Lowry signs gaming compact

1994   *U.S. v. Washington* (Judge Rafeedie upholds tribal right to shellfish)

1994   Gray whale removed from endangered species list

1994   Self-governance becomes permanent law

1994   Memorandum on Government-to-Government Relations

1996   Executive Order 13007 protects sacred sites on federal lands

1999   First successful Makah whale hunt since 1921

Key to Pronunciation

There are several ways in which native-language words appear in this book. The standardized phonetic alphabet below is the form used most often. However, tribal-language programs have developed various ways to accommodate manual typewriters and computers that do not have special characters. The Skokomish have developed their own unique system. Other tribes sometimes use the English alphabet to attempt to capture unique language sounds; this makes typing easier but pronunciation less accurate.

Approximate English values for the standardized phonetic alphabet appear below.

ʔ	Glottal Stop, as in Oh-oh!
a	f<u>a</u>ther
c	ha<u>ts</u>
č	<u>ch</u>urch
e	y<u>e</u>t
ə	sof<u>a</u> or j<u>u</u>st
i	mach<u>i</u>ne
kʷ	<u>qu</u>it
ɫ	p<u>l</u>ay
λ	a<u>tl</u>as
ŋ	lu<u>ng</u>
q	<u>c</u>all
qʷ	<u>qu</u>alm
u	between r<u>u</u>le and j<u>o</u>ke
š	Engli<u>sh</u>
w	to<u>w</u>er
xʷ	<u>wh</u>ich
x	<u>h</u>uge

Ejectives below are "ejected" out of the mouth with a loud pop.

p̓, t̓, c̓, č̓, k̓, q̓, k̓ʷ, q̓ʷ

Timothy Montler, of the University of North Texas, Denton, provided the phonetics font program used in this volume.

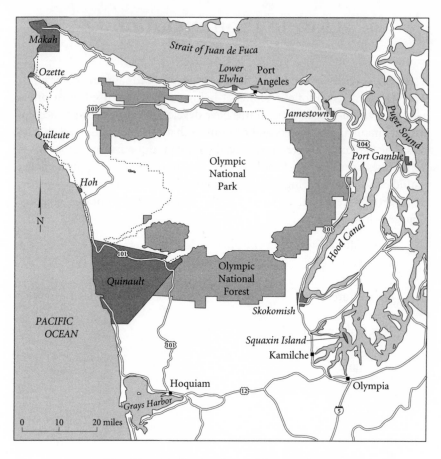

The Olympic Peninsula and Reservations

NATIVE PEOPLES
of the
Olympic Peninsula

Introduction

The Olympic Peninsula forms the extreme northwest corner of Washington State and the conterminous United States. The glacier-clad Olympic Mountains rise from the center of the peninsula. Rivers and streams drain from these mountains into the surrounding marine waters of the Strait of Juan de Fuca to the north, Hood Canal to the east, Grays Harbor to the south, and the Pacific Ocean to the west.

Through time the peninsula has remained relatively isolated from the rest of the continental mainland because of changes in sea level and ice cover. About 15,000 years ago the Olympic Peninsula was covered with ice to the north and east, and the western coastline extended twelve to thirty miles farther offshore than it does today. A glacial refugia, or ice-free zone, existed south of the present town of Forks and may have been inhabited by people before the continental ice sheet began its retreat on the western peninsula about 14,500 years ago (Heusser 1973).

As a result of the peninsula's relative isolation from the rest of Washington, thirty-five unique species of plants, insects, fish, mollusks, and amphibians are endemic to the Olympic Peninsula. Among these species are Flett's violet (*Viola flettii*), the Olympic grasshopper (*Nisquallia olympica*), the Beardslee rainbow trout (*Oncorhynchus mykiss beardsleei*), and the Olympic marmot (*Marmota olympus*).

As the glaciers began to retreat, people moved into the newly opened areas. The present-day Indian tribes of the Olympic Peninsula region represented in this book—beginning due north on the Strait of Juan de Fuca and moving clockwise—include the Elwha Klallam, Jamestown S'Klallam, Port Gamble S'Klallam, Skokomish, Squaxin Island, Quinault, Hoh, Quileute, and Makah. Tribal reservation lands on the peninsula comprise more than 220,000 acres, ranging from the Quinault Reservation, embracing 212,000 acres, to the Jamestown S'Klallam Reservation, with only 21 acres.

Most western Washington tribal languages derive from the Salishan language family, yet on the Olympic Peninsula there are three distinct language families: Salishan, Chimakuan, and Wakashan. The Klallam, Quinault, and Twana languages, spoken by the S'Klallam, Quinault, and Skokomish respectively, are Salishan. The Squaxin Island and other Puget Sound languages are Lushootseed, a closely related Salishan language. The Makah language is part of the Nootkan branch of the Wakashan language family. The nearest linguistic relatives of the Makah are the Nootka and Nitinat on the west coast of Vancouver Island. The Hoh and Quileute language is called Quileute, one of only two languages in the Chimakuan language family. The Chemakum people, who once lived in the northeastern portion of the peninsula from Port Townsend to the entrance of Hood Canal, spoke the other Chimakuan language. Many people spoke more than one language and also used the regional trade language, Chinook Jargon.

Each of the peninsula tribes had unique native-language names for themselves, for their villages, for geologic landmarks, and for the many places they regarded as culturally significant. Beginning in the 1700s, these names began

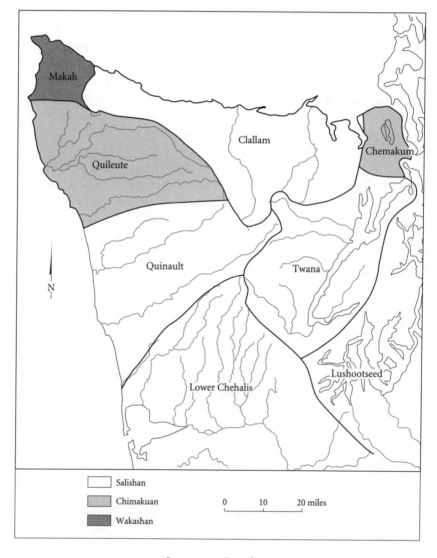

Language Families

Olympic Mountains. Courtesy of North Olympic Library, Kellogg Collection.

to be replaced with names given by Spanish and English explorers. The English-speaking settlers named rivers, towns, and landforms by adopting or altering many traditional Indian names. Examples are Bogachiel, Calawah, Copalis, Dickey, Dosewallips, Duckabush, Ennis, Hamma Hamma, Hoko, Kitsap, Neah, Quilcene, Pysht, Sekiu, Sequim, Snahapish, Toleak, and Tshletshy.

The relationship between the first people and the Olympic Peninsula is recounted in origin legends and mythic events that explain both the creation of the landscape and people's relationship to it. These legends depict a reliance on waterways, forests, and valleys for the acquisition of vital resources and give detailed descriptions of travel into the mountains for pleasure, social interchange such as marriage, and spiritual pursuits.

Early explorers and some historians have asserted that village settlements and resource locations were found only along the lower valleys and marine shorelines; some have even characterized American Indians as being afraid to go into the mountains. This perception is probably based on the fact that most immigrants had very little firsthand knowledge or interest in the interior of the peninsula until the 1890s, and the early explorers wanted to portray themselves as the first to enter the area. Recent archaeological and archival research supports what tribal spoken history tells us about the extensive use of the peninsula's interior reaches. These areas were and continue to be a part of tribal lifeways, that is, "the systems of values and practices that guide community subsistence and spiritual relationships with the environment, ways of organizing family and community life, and ways of celebrating life and mourning death"(Scovill 1987: 20).

All of the peninsula tribes tell of the Great Flood that rose many generations ago above all but a few Olympic Mountain peaks. The Quileute account is as follows:

> Thunderbird was very angry one time. He caused the ocean to rise. . . . The waters rose for four days. They rose until the very tops of the mountains were covered with water. . . . There was no sun. There was no land. For four days the water receded. But now the people were much scattered. (Reagan and Walters 1933: 322)

Great Flood traditions are also widespread among tribes well beyond the Olympic Peninsula. It is possible that some of these accounts relate to the retreat of the continental glaciers about fifteen thousand years ago. More recent events may refer to tsunamis from postglacial earthquakes in the region.

One tsunami in Puget Sound about one thousand years ago resulted from a large earthquake on the Seattle fault (Atwater and Moore 1992). Another tsunami along the Pacific Coast was triggered by an earthquake of magnitude 8.0 or larger between August 1699 and May 1700 (Yamaguchi 1997). This tsunami crossed the Pacific Ocean to Japan, where official documents record scattered damage from a tsunami of distant origin in late January 1700 along six hundred miles of Honshu's Pacific coastline (Atwater et al. 1999; Satake et al. 1996). Sand and other deposits from tsunamis cover archaeological sites in southern Washington and northern Oregon (Cole et al. 1996; Minor and Grant 1996). Geologists are currently conducting research relating the oral history of this region to earthquakes and tidal events.

Archaeological research suggests that as the glaciers receded, people moved into the high country, where new vegetation attracted game and expanded hunting and gathering opportunities (Bergland 1983; Schalk 1988). The remains of stone tool manufacture, called lithic materials, have been documented in the Olympic Mountains and surrounding foothills. Archaeologists have also uncovered hearth sites, where meals were cooked between four thousand and eight thousand years ago, near mountain lakes, ridgelines, marshes, and meadows. These sites feature the stone tools and associated manufacturing debris—used for hunting, butchering, and plant processing—that increase knowledge about this hunting and gathering lifestyle (Conca and Haertel 1995).

In 1993 fragments of a neatly woven basket were found in the alpine reaches of Olympic National Park, providing additional evidence of high country habitation. These fragments were part of a basket that was used as a backpack. A radiocarbon date of 2880+/-70 B.P. (before the present) has been determined for the basket. Previously, archaeologists believed it was less than

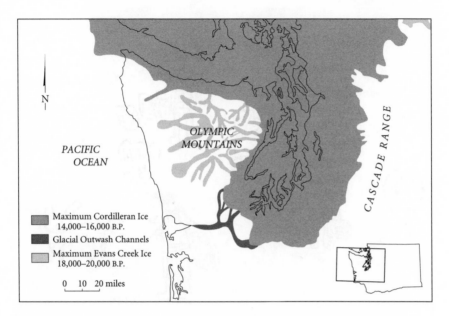

Glaciation

five hundred years old, so this is important information that supports tribal knowledge of their long connection to the mountains of the peninsula.

On the northern peninsula, the retreating glaciers left a landscape of marsh- and grasslands that attracted large animals including mastodons, caribou, elk, and bison. In 1977 the earliest archaeological evidence of human presence on the peninsula was found at a site near Sequim, where the 12,000-year-old remains of a mastodon showed signs of human butchering with stone tools (Gustafson et al. 1979).

Archaeological excavations in 1996, during construction preparation for Highway 101 in Sequim, led to the discovery of two sites. The first appears to date between 8000 and 6000 B.P. and is a site where people obtained cobbles from an old channel of the Dungeness River to make stone tools. The other site has been radiocarbon dated at between 2600 and 170 B.P. and provides evidence that people occupied temporary houses (there are two house pits) where they processed deer and elk as well as hazelnuts and berries for winter storage. It is likely that ancestors of the S'Klallam occupied these houses, as well as villages along Sequim Bay and the Strait of Juan de Fuca (Morgan 1998).

Between 3000 and 1000 B.P., river and ocean fisheries and other maritime economies became increasingly important, as populations grew and commerce among groups expanded. Middens found at the mouth of the Hoko River on the Strait of Juan de Fuca contain skeletal remains of halibut, cod, and salmon, which indicate that this location was used for offshore fishing.

Drawing of pack basket by Dorothy Gurerro, Quileute Tribe.

The pursuit of fish along the Strait of Juan de Fuca was made possible by a cedar woodworking technology that included canoe manufacture (Bergland and Marr 1988).

The Ozette archaeological site is a village location on the Pacific Coast. Although there were a few remaining residents here until the 1930s, the site itself dates between 1000 and 200 B.P. The Ozette community had an economy based on specialized fishing, sealing, and whaling. This site has provided archaeologists with the opportunity to study a large maritime village (see the chapter on the Makah). There are several other archaeological sites on the outer coast that reflect similar use.

At sites near Vancouver, British Columbia, porpoise and other sea mammal remains suggest that watercraft technology may have been in use between 9000 and 4500 B.P. (Matson and Coupland 1995: 81). The people of the Olympic Peninsula used many types of canoes suited to a variety of conditions—open seas, bays, and rivers—for travel, fishing, hunting, and transport. The canoes were poled upriver as far as possible and were also kept on navigable portions of rivers above obstructions. According to the anthropologist Ronald Olson (1936: 87), "At log jams portages were constructed, skids being used for sliding the canoe. Log jams were usually burned during the summer in order to keep the channel open."

Trails were used where canoes could not go, following the river drainages to the open meadows and mountain ridgelines. Trails crossed the mountains between the Chahlatt (Hoh) and Elwha Rivers and from the Quileute to the Pysht and the Hoko (Gibbs [1855]1877: 167). Other trails led from Hood Canal to Grays Harbor and crossed the Olympics from the Skokomish and Dosewallips River drainages to the Quinault. Many of the trail routes are used today by hikers in Olympic National Park and the Olympic National Forest.

The Quileute word for early European voyagers who traveled along the outer Pacific Coast is Hokwat', which means "drifting house people." The word *poston* or *pástəd* is also used to refer to Europeans. This is a Chinook

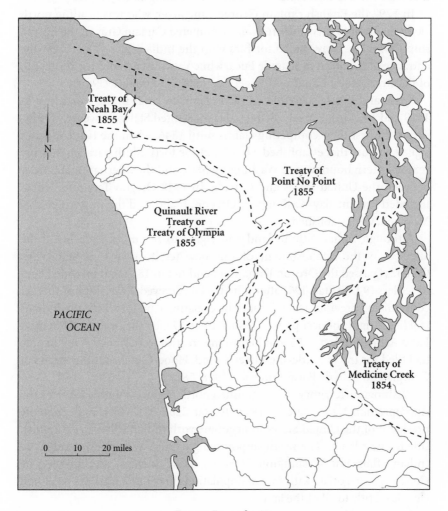

Treaty Boundaries

Jargon term first used to describe John Jacob Astor's traders who came from Boston in 1811. Astor's company founded Astoria, on the Columbia River, as the first permanent U.S. settlement on the northwest coast.

It is probable that some native communities, particularly those along the Pacific shoreline of the peninsula, met the Hokwat' before the first recorded Spanish landing of the Bruno de Hezeta–Juan Francisco de la Bodega y Quadra Expedition near the Quinault River in 1775. Exploration of the Northwest Coast began in the late 1500s; however, the region did not become a focus for Spanish, Russian, French, British, and American traders and explorers until the late 1700s. Each of these newcomers laid claim to lands that were the territories and homelands of the indigenous people.

In 1792 the English captain George Vancouver, who was heading north along the coast to survey the region, encountered Captain Gray of the Boston ship *Columbia*. Gray traded for furs with the Indians at a village near the entrance of the Strait of Juan de Fuca, while Vancouver traced the shorelines of the strait, Hood Canal, and Puget Sound (Whitebrook 1959: 70).

Spain and Russia surrendered their claims to lands in the Northwest in 1819 and 1824 respectively. Britain and the United States, however, continued to contest their competing claims until 1846, when the two countries signed a treaty that established a border at the forty-ninth parallel, the current northern boundary of Washington State and the international border between the United States and Canada. In 1848 Oregon Territory, which included present-day Washington, Oregon, Idaho, and the western part of Montana, was established.

Although Indian title to land and rights to resources were not to be affected by the establishment of this new territory (9 U.S. Stat. 323), Congress passed the Oregon Donation Land Act in 1850 that provided land to settlers (9 U.S. Stat. 496) after it had been surveyed. Provisions of this act contradicted previous federal policy by donating land for which the Indians still held "rights of occupancy" (Asher 1999: 37). By the time the Donation Land Act expired in 1855 and before the treaties were signed, "529 people had filed for tracts bordering Puget Sound, Hood Canal, and the Straits of Georgia and Juan de Fuca" (Harmon 1998: 58).

Washington Territory was established north of the Columbia River by the Appropriation Act of March 3, 1853 (10 Stat. 226, 238), which authorized the president of the United States to negotiate with Indian tribes to extinguish title to their lands. The newly appointed governor and superintendent of Indian affairs for Washington Territory, Isaac Stevens, was directed by Congress to negotiate with Indian populations in the new territory to obtain clear legal title to all of the land.

Stevens and his treaty commission first negotiated the Treaty of Medicine

Creek, signed on December 26, 1854, by the people from Squaxin Island and several other Puget Sound groups, including the Nisqually and Puyallup. The Treaty of Point No Point, the first of the Olympic Peninsula treaties, was made with the S'Klallam, Twana, Skokomish, and Chemakum on January 25, 1855. The Treaty of Neah Bay was made with the Makah and Ozette and signed on January 31, 1855. After a failed treaty negotiation with the Chehalis, Chinook, Cowlitz, Quinault, and Queets in March 1855, a later treaty was made with the Quinault, Queets, Quileute, and Hoh. This, the last of the Stevens treaties in western Washington, known both as the Treaty of Olympia and as the Quinault River Treaty, was signed on July 1, 1855, on the Quinault River by Indian agent Michael Simmons on behalf of Stevens and by Governor Stevens on January 25, 1856 in Olympia. Tribal representatives who agreed to the treaties ceded their lands to the United States only after assurances that they could continue fishing, hunting, and gathering in their traditional territories. Just a fraction of their ceded lands were retained as reservation land.

Stevens and his treaty commission were aware that village leaders did not have authority beyond their families and friends. These leaders were people who excelled in qualities such as diplomacy, fishing, hunting, house building, or warfare, but they were not looked to for guidance and leadership by other villages. Therefore, Stevens carried out the treaty process by designating "tribes and chiefs" to unite the independent villages (Harmon 1998: 79).

Under the terms of the treaties, reservations were established on the Olympic Peninsula at Neah Bay, Taholah, and Skokomish. The Medicine Creek Treaty provided a reservation on Squaxin Island (Klah-Che-Min). The people were expected to leave their villages and move their permanent homes to the reservations. This plan was especially painful for those whose homelands and resource areas were far away from the reservations. In the late 1800s small reservations were established by executive order for the Quileute (1889), Hoh (1893), and Ozette (1893). It was not until much later that the three S'Klallam reservations were proclaimed.

The tribes were to be compensated for their lands; however, most were paid negligible amounts. The Indian Claims Commission (60 U.S. Stat. 1049) was established in 1946 to resolve inadequate compensation claims. To receive compensation for their lands, the tribes had to prove exclusive use and occupancy.

Although there are some differences, all of the treaties specify that the tribes have the right to fish at "usual and accustomed grounds and stations . . . in common with all citizens . . . together with the privilege of hunting and gathering roots and berries on open and unclaimed lands" (Treaty of Point No Point and Treaty of Neah Bay 1855; Treaty of Olympia 1856; Treaty of Medicine Creek 1854). In the 1974 case *U.S. v. Washington*, federal district

Quinault fisherman, Ed Boldt, and his boat, 1998. Courtesy of Quinault Indian Nation Community Relations.

court judge George Boldt interpreted the words "in common with" to mean that the Indians were guaranteed an equal share or half of the sustainable harvest of anadromous fish. Judge Boldt found that the treaties were "not a grant of rights to the Indians, but a grant of rights from them, and a reservation of those not granted." The tribes' right to fish was not given to them through the treaties with the United States; this was a right they had had from time immemorial. In signing the treaties, the tribes agreed to share their fishery resources with the newcomers to what would soon become Washington State.

To make his enduring decision defining the tribes' rights to harvest fish in western Washington in all areas they had used before signing the treaties and to co-manage the fishery resource with the state of Washington, Judge Boldt relied upon the credible evidence presented by Dr. Barbara Lane, the U.S. government's expert witness. The Boldt decision became the landmark case regarding treaty rights. The U.S. Supreme Court affirmed *U.S. v. Washington* in 1979.

U.S. district court judge Edward Rafeedie ruled in December 1994 that the western Washington treaty tribes have the right to harvest 50 percent of the harvestable shellfish on tidelands under specified terms and conditions. In February 1998 the U.S. Ninth Circuit Court of Appeals reaffirmed Rafeedie's ruling. Then in April 1999 the U.S. Supreme Court announced that it would not hear appeals of the case that reaffirmed these harvesting rights.

Tribes and the Federal Government

Several issues of tribal-federal government relationships are presented here to provide a clearer understanding of the fiduciary or trust responsibility of the federal government.

EDUCATION

The Stevens treaties specified that the federal government would provide an agricultural and industrial school at the general agency for Puget Sound within one year. This did not happen as promised, but in 1876 the federal government began to appropriate funds specifically for Indian education, "apart from support promised in treaties" (Hagan 1988: 59). Several Indian day schools were established on the Olympic Peninsula in the years after the treaty. The teachers at these schools were often missionaries or employees of the Indian agency and enforced harsh changes in tribal lifeways, such as restricting the speaking of native languages, assigning new Christian names to replace given names, and teaching Christian religion while prohibiting native religious practices.

A new government school was built at Tulalip in 1905, and in 1910 the agency superintendent, Charles Buchanan, reported that the school fulfilled the treaty promise for a central agency school (Harmon 1998: 166). By this time the federal government had already established a number of boarding schools. Many peninsula tribal members attended the first off-reservation boarding school in the Northwest, Chemawa, established at Salem, Oregon, in 1880.

In the 1920s a review of Bureau of Indian Affairs (BIA) policies, including education, resulted in a report titled *The Problem of Indian Administration* (Meriam 1928). This report scrutinized Indian education and resulted in reforms of the inadequate boarding school system. Many boarding schools were closed, but a few, including Chemawa, were improved and remained open (Szasz and Ryan 1988: 294). The chapter on the Elwha Klallam discusses the positive experience of two tribal elders who attended Chemawa after Indian education had been improved.

In 1934 the Johnson-O'Malley Act (48 U.S. Stat. 596) was designed to enable states to administer BIA funding for Indian education. However, the funding was used for general school programs and did not fulfill the intended goal of addressing Indian student needs. In 1975 the Indian Self-Determination and Education Assistance Act (88 U.S. Stat. 2203) directed funding for Johnson-O'Malley programs to tribes to meet Indian educational goals (Szasz and Ryan 1988: 294, 298). The tribes on the peninsula have since implemented many valuable tribal education programs on their reservations and in cooperation with public schools.

TRIBES

The term "tribe" is generally used by the federal government to define "a group of Indians who share a common heritage and speak a distinct language" (Pevar 1992: 14). The federal government recognizes 558 Indian tribes and Alaska Native corporations; 28 tribes are recognized in Washington State. Today tribes that are not recognized by the federal government must complete a legal process to obtain federal acknowledgment. In 1978 the BIA implemented regulations to officially acknowledge tribal entities (25 CFR 54). The Jamestown S'Klallam chapter discusses the procedure they followed to become federally recognized in 1981.

Tribes are recognized as sovereign entities by the federal government. Article 6 of the U.S. Constitution recognizes that a treaty between sovereigns "is the supreme law of the land." In 1871 Congress stopped negotiating treaties with tribes as sovereigns, and actions that formerly required negotiations with the tribe were carried out directly by Congress (16 U.S. Stat. 566). This did not affect treaties ratified before 1871 (Hagan 1988: 55–56). Since that time tribes have struggled to assert their right to self-governance as sovereigns.

The Indian Reorganization Act (IRA) of 1934 (48 U.S. Stat. 984–986) was considered by Congress the foundation for the future of tribal self-determination. Tribes could choose to accept the IRA, which included formalizing a tribal constitution through a council and an executive or advisory committee. The IRA provided for the purchase of land for landless Indians, which was especially important for the S'Klallam tribes.

The federal government has a trust responsibility to forward the interests of federally recognized tribes. This relationship is based on the promises made to the tribes in treaties and congressional acts to protect their interests and well-being. Stressing the importance of this federal trust responsibility, President Bill Clinton issued a memorandum on April 29, 1994, titled "Government-to-Government Relations with Native American Tribal Governments" (U.S. Government 1994). The relationship is set forth in the U.S. Constitution and in treaties, statutes, and court decisions. This memorandum outlines the need for federal agencies to consult with tribes before taking actions that may affect them.

Significant legislation to protect tribal interests includes the 1990 Native American Graves Protection and Repatriation Act (NAGPRA), which requires federal agencies and museums to inventory their collections and establish the affiliation of cultural items. This law also stipulates protection of Native American graves and cultural items on federal lands (P.L. 101-601, November 16, 1990).

The American Indian Religious Freedom Act (AIRFA) (P.L. 95-341, August 11, 1978) was enacted to protect and preserve the right to believe, express, and exercise traditional Native American religions. This includes access to sites, use and possession of sacred objects, and worship through ceremonial and traditional rites. Unfortunately, AIRFA does not have any enforceable provisions. To strengthen the federal government's role in the protection of tribal sacred places, President Clinton issued Executive Order 13007 on May 24, 1996, which calls for the development of policies and procedures to protect Indian sacred sites on federal lands.

The National Historic Preservation Act (NHPA) of 1966 as amended (16 U.S.C. 470) recognizes important cultural sites, structures, and landscapes, as well as traditional religious and cultural areas. NHPA specifies that tribes and federal agencies work together on historic preservation in the form of identification, evaluation, and protection of historic properties, places that are eligible for the National Register of Historic Places. A traditional cultural property is evaluated for eligibility for the National Register based on traditional practices and beliefs. Some sites may never be classified as historic properties because they are so important and sacred they are known only to certain tribal members.

The tribes of the Olympic Peninsula retain strong cultural traditions and are working to record and maintain their languages and train their children in traditional skills. They also look forward to a future of cultural preservation and sharing knowledge with others, not only about their language and heritage, but to create an understanding of the unique place they occupy in the United States as distinct peoples with recognized tribal governments. The indigenous people of the Olympic Peninsula are members of the total community and wish to see their heritage respected and understood.

The chapters that follow present tribal perspectives on contemporary activities important to the tribes today. None of the chapters is a complete history. It is for this reason that each chapter concludes with suggested reading.

SUGGESTED READING

Cohen, Fay G. 1986. *Treaties on Trial: The Continuing Controversy over Northwest Indian Fishing Rights.* Seattle: University of Washington Press.

Pevar, Stephen L. 1992. *The Rights of Indians and Tribes. The Basic ACLU Guide to Indian and Tribal Rights.* Carbondale: Southern Illinois University Press.

Suttles, Wayne, ed. 1990. *Handbook of North American Indians.* Vol. 7: *The Northwest Coast.* Washington D.C.: Smithsonian Institution Press.

The S'Klallam:

Elwha, Jamestown,

and Port Gamble

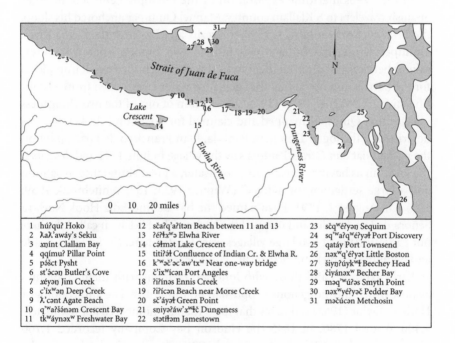

1 húʔquʔ Hoko
2 ƛaƛ̓awáy's Sekiu
3 x̣mínt Clallam Bay
4 qqímuʔ Pillar Point
5 pə́sct Pysht
6 st'ə́cən Butler's Cove
7 x̣éyəŋ Jim Creek
8 c'íx̣ʷən Deep Creek
9 ƛ̓cənt Agate Beach
10 q'ʷaʔšə́nəm Crescent Bay
11 tkʷáynəx̣ʷ Freshwater Bay

12 sčaʔq'aʔítən Beach between 11 and 13
13 ʔéʔɬx̣ʷə Elwha River
14 cə́ɬmət Lake Crescent
15 titiʔə́ɬ Confluence of Indian Cr. & Elwha R.
16 k̓ʷəč'əc'aw'txʷ Near one-way bridge
17 č'ix̣ʷícən Port Angeles
18 ʔiʔínəs Ennis Creek
19 ʔiʔícən Beach near Morse Creek
20 sč'áyəɬ Green Point
21 sniyəʔáw'x̣ʷɬč Dungeness
22 stətíɬəm Jamestown

23 sčqʷéʔyəŋ Sequim
24 sqʷaʔqʷéʔyəɬ Port Discovery
25 qatáy Port Townsend
26 nəxʷq'éʔyət Little Boston
27 šiynʔúykʷɬ Beechey Head
28 čiyánəxʷ Becher Bay
29 məqʷúʔəs Smyth Point
30 nəxʷyéʔyəč Pedder Bay
31 məčúcən Metchosin

S'Klallam Village Sites
Elwha Klallam Tribe (Montler 1995)

Historically, the S'Klallam lived throughout the northern Olympic Peninsula and were united by language and kinship. Today they are divided politically into three reservations: the Elwha Klallam, the Jamestown S'Klallam, and the Port Gamble S'Klallam. There are various spellings of the word *S'Klallam*. The Jamestown and Port Gamble use the spelling S'Klallam as it appears in the 1855 treaty. The Elwha Klallam omit the *S'*. In this volume the word is spelled S'Klallam, unless referring to the Elwha Klallam specifically or the Klallam language.

S'Klallam is an anglicized version *nəxʷsƛáy'əm'*, which according to tradition means "strong (or mighty) people." The Klallam language is of the Central Salish branch of the Salishan linguistic family. The S'Klallam are most closely related linguistically to the Sooke, Songish, and Saanich Canadian First Nations on southeastern Vancouver Island and to the Lummi Tribe near Bellingham, Washington.

In the 1790s maritime exploration of the Olympic Peninsula brought Spanish travelers to S'Klallam country. Manuel Quimper anchored his sloop, the *Princesa Real*, on July 21, 1790, in Freshwater Bay near the Elwha River. Quimper wrote that Indians met him in two canoes, offered the crew salmonberries, and directed them to freshwater. He traded small iron pieces for the berries and noted that the "delicious water [was] taken from a beautiful stream" (Wagner 1933: 119). A description of one of the two Dungeness villages that Quimper mapped and claimed for Spain on July 4, 1790, was described in the log of Don Juan Pantoja, Juan Francisco de Eliza's pilot on the packetboat *San Carlos*. Pantoja saw the village in June 1791 and described the location as having "streams of good water, a great abundance of salmon and a large settlement of natives" (Wagner 1933: 189; Whitebrook 1959: 107). On August 2, 1791, Eliza named the bay behind Ediz Hook Nuestra Señora de Los Angeles and mapped the harbor. The S'Klallam called the harbor *č'xʷicən*. At least two large villages were located here, *č'xʷicən* (lit., inside and behind; the spit) and *ʔiʔínəs* (lit., good beach).

Early explorers and those who followed brought with them epidemics against which the indigenous people had no immunity. The anthropologist Herbert Taylor (1963) estimates that the S'Klallam numbered approximately 2,400 around 1780. In 1845 the Hudson Bay Company recorded 1,760 S'Klallam, and by 1855 there were only 926. This drastic decline was the result of smallpox, whooping cough, and measles (Eells 1887: 272).

Each S'Klallam village functioned as a semiautonomous group, although intervillage relationships and kinship ties were strong. With the advent of immigrant homesteading in the area, S'Klallam lands were taken, and fewer, more central villages were occupied (BIA 1980: 2).

The S'Klallam, along with the Chemakum and Skokomish, were signatories to the 1855 Treaty of Point No Point. In signing the treaty to cede 438,430 acres of S'Klallam territory to the federal government, the S'Klallam understood that a reservation was to be established for them between Sequim and Dungeness Bay. Treaty journal notes show a reservation was considered "on the straits" (BIA 1980: 5). Indian agent Michael Simmons recommended in 1859 that the "Clallams, living on the Straits of Fuca [sic], be allowed a reserve at Clallam Bay" (ARCIA 1860: 398). However, no reservation was established and they were informed they had to move onto the Skokomish Reservation. Most S'Klallam refused to move from their usual and accustomed fishing areas and traditional homeland (BIA 1980: 6).

There was a concerted effort by the BIA to organize the S'Klallam under the Indian Reorganization Act (IRA) of 1934 (48 U.S. Stat. 984) and provide them with reservation land. The first proposal was to combine the three S'Klallam bands, and the second was to organize the Jamestown and Elwha separately from the Port Gamble; however, all efforts to consolidate the tribes were abandoned in the late 1930s (BIA 1980: 13), and today the three S'Klallam tribes are distinct federally recognized tribes with separate reservations.

Elwha tribal members Romana Benke and Michael Langland featured in
mural painted by Cory Ench. Elwha Klallam Tribe.

Elwha Klallam

Jamie Valadez

The Elwha Klallam were created at a place on the Elwha River where the Creator bathed and blessed them. There are holes in the rocks here that are called *spčúʔ*, which means "coiled baskets." An early account by the ethnologist T. T. Waterman (1920: 58) describes this spot: "The pits or hollows are the place from which dirt was scooped, out of which the human race was formed. Sometimes people go to these pits to get information about their future life. If a man thrusts his hand into this water, and brings out deer-hair for example, he knows he will be a good hunter."

Cultural History

The Klallam people are traditionally known as "the strong people." In the 1930s tribal elder Sam Ulmer related the story that explains how this name came to be used. It is retold by Beatrice Charles:

> One day there was a big gathering at Elwha. The people ate salmon, clams, wild berries, and lots of good things from nature. At the time a longhouse was being built and they decided to see who could get the big log to the roof. "Who can lift this big log?" the speaker asked. All of the other tribes tried to lift it, with no success. Then it was time for the mighty Klallams. Knowing that logs float, they rolled the log into the water. Then their strongest men walked out into the water and they let the log float onto their shoulders. When they walked out of the water they were carrying the log on their shoulders. Upon reaching the longhouse, everyone shouted at the same time, "Shashume, Shashume, Shashume"[1] and on the third Shashume they all lifted the log to the top. The other tribes thought that the mighty Klallams must be very strong to put the log up so high and also so smart to use the water to first get the log onto their shoulders. They all shouted, "Klallam, Klallam!" which means "Strong People!" That was how our tribe received its name so long ago.

The Elwha River is home to Thunderbird, an important symbol of strength to the Klallam people. Thunderbird lived in a cave and chased the salmon upriver by sending thunder and lightning toward the mouth of the Elwha. When the lightning hit the water it turned into a two-headed serpent called čínak̓ʷə. Then the Klallam prepared to fish, because they knew a good run of fish was coming. Thunderbird helped the people in this way.

Another important symbol to the Klallam is Killer Whale, q̓ʰúməčən. As told by Adeline Smith, a Klallam man named Pysht Jack had a widowed relative with several children, and he always helped her. During this time, Victoria was the city where the Indians went to trade. Pysht Jack's relative caught many fish, and they would travel to Victoria to trade her salmon. On one trip the weather turned very stormy as they were crossing the strait, and they both thought they were going to drown. The woman started praying and chanting for the q̓ʰúməčən to help them. There were only certain people who could call on the q̓ʰúməčən, and she was one who had that power. It was not long before several q̓ʰúməčən appeared. The killer whales surrounded the canoe and safely escorted them across the strait to the mouth of the Elwha River. The woman thanked the q̓ʰúməčən and they swam away, and that is why the Klallam people say that the q̓ʰúməčən is their protector. Both the Thunderbird and Killer Whale are depicted in the tribe's logo.

It has been a common misperception that the Klallam did not travel into the mountains. Klallam families not only traveled up and over the Olympic Mountains to gather medicinal plants, berries, bear grass, and cattails and to hunt for bear, deer, and elk; they also lived in upriver villages on a seasonal basis and in some places year-round. The Elwha was a natural byway for subsistence activities, but also for social gatherings. One Klallam mother hiked up the Elwha and over to Taholah at the mouth of the Quinault River every summer with her five children to visit relatives there. The Klallam consider the Olympic Mountains sacred and revere the mountains' glory.

Klallam ties to the mountains date back to the Great Flood many generations ago, as Joe Sampson describes:

> There was a man who told his people to make some canoes and to make them large and strong so they could endure storms. There was a flood coming. The people said the mountains were high and they could just go up the mountains when the flood came. He warned them again. Soon it began to rain and rained for many days. And the rivers became salt. The people said they would go up the mountains. . . . They had no way of getting to the mountains for the valleys were full of water and the rivers overflowed their banks.
>
> The people that walked all died. Those that had canoes and water and food lived. Some who were in a canoe tied themselves to a treetop when their canoe

hit the trees and split. Many died. Some tied themselves to mountains and the highest ones were saved. (Gunther 1925: 119)

One of the mountains that saved the Klallam has been described by many people and appears to be either Mount Carrie or Mount Olympus. Mount Carrie, closer and clearly visible from Elwha, is the more likely of the two.

A Klallam man named *wəqínəxən*, or Boston Charlie, used to hunt elk in the Olympic Mountains. He spent his summers in the mountains and had favorite camping spots that he frequented until he was very old. One of his campsites is a contemporary hiking destination near Mount Carrie called Boston Charlie's Camp. Many local people relate accounts of Boston's mountain expeditions.

Boston Charlie was the last medicine man of the Klallam people and would go up to the Olympic Hot Springs for spiritual cleansing, long before the springs were known to white settlers. In his later years, Boston was six days late returning from the mountains, and his family sent out a search party. They found him lying on the side of a hill. Boston told how he was lost, hungry, and thirsty and could go no farther. He was lying at the top of a precipice when *čičayík*ʷ*tən*, a mountain being similar to Sasquatch, appeared from the side of the cliff offering a large thimbleberry leaf full of berries with dew on them. This gave him the energy and fluids he needed to continue until his nephews found him and helped him home.

In 1847 the Canadian artist Paul Kane crossed the Strait of Juan de Fuca from Victoria and visited the Klallam village of *ʔiʔínəs* at Ennis Creek east of Port Angeles harbor. Kane made several drawings and paintings of the Klallam, including this village. His painting of *ʔiʔínəs* was used as a model for the 1997 mural on the Arthur D. Feiro Marine Life Center at the Port Angeles City Pier, which is shown on page 20.

Historically, ancestors of the Elwha Klallam Tribe lived in villages on both sides of the Strait of Juan de Fuca. On the north side of the strait near Victoria was the Klallam village of Beecher Bay. On the peninsula there were Klallam villages at Hoko, Clallam Bay, Pysht, Deep Creek, Freshwater Bay, the Elwha valley and river mouth, the shores of Port Angeles (False Dungeness), and creeks farther east.

When the Treaty of Point No Point was signed in 1855, the Klallam refused to move onto the Skokomish Reservation on Hood Canal. They preferred to remain in their own villages near their fishing and gathering places and where their ancestors were laid to rest.

Settlers began arriving in the lower Elwha valley in the 1860s. Port Angeles and other towns were established at about the same time. The homesteaders pushed many Klallam from their traditional homesites. Some

Hartley Goodwin (left) and *wəqínəxən* (right), who was called Boston
Charlie because he had adopted some ways of the whites early on
and was one of the Klallam who homesteaded in the Elwha valley.
Courtesy of Adeline Smith.

Klallam purchased land at Clallam Bay and Port Angeles but found that because they were not considered U.S. citizens, they were unable to obtain title to their ancestral holdings. With the passage of the 1884 Indian Homestead Act, several Klallam families eventually became landowners. By 1894 there were ten Klallam families who held trust patents to their land, amounting to about thirteen hundred acres in the Elwha valley and at Freshwater Bay. Six of these homesteads were located along the Elwha River and are now part of the Elwha Klallam Reservation; the others are no longer held by Klallam tribal members.

In taking up homesteads, the Klallam (and other tribes) were required to sever tribal relations. Many did not want to do this and therefore had to leave their homesites. Landless Klallam families moved to the rocky shores west of the Elwha River or to Ediz Hook (Morrison 1939: 17).

Indian homesteaders adapted to the altered circumstances, taking up new occupations, clearing and fencing farms, planting orchards, and selling work oxen, pigs, potatoes, oats, fuel, and other products, as well as continuing to supply fish and game to markets and individuals in the region. The Elwha River fishery remained the mainstay of the economy, both for the Klallam who continued to fish for a living and for those who worked in the woods and mills. Not all Klallam changed the way they made a living, however. As one elder explained, "You can't make farmers out of fisherman."

The main source of food for the Klallam has always been obtained by fishing. All five species of salmon were harvested in the Elwha River until 1910, when construction of the first of two dams was begun. The lower dam was completed in 1914, which prevented the salmon from returning to their spawning grounds, leaving thousands of fish to die below the dams. In 1910 state law required a license to fish; however, tribal members could not obtain a license because they were not considered U.S. citizens. The Elwha Klallam would gather the dead fish below the dams, but even possession of dead fish resulted in jail sentences (Morrison 1939: 18). Elders today recall their childhood years when they would sneak down to the river to fish because their families had no food. They tied the fish with twine and dragged them through the fields of tall grass to avoid the game wardens. In 1924 American Indians became U.S. citizens, but their fishing rights continued to be restricted by the state.

On June 18, 1934, the Wheeler-Howard Act, or Indian Reorganization Act, was passed. According to President Franklin D. Roosevelt, the bill was intended to provide the "opportunity for self-determination for the Indians in handling their property by providing modern corporate management, participation in local government, a more liberal education system through day schools and advanced health measures" (Morrison 1939: 10).

On March 8, 1934, the Northwest Indian Conference met at Chemawa Indian boarding school to discuss the proposed IRA with high-level Bureau of Indian Affairs (BIA) officials. Members of tribes from Washington, Oregon, Idaho, and Montana participated in the discussions, and Chemawa students took the minutes. One of these students was LaVerne Hepfer, daughter of Sam Ulmer, a Klallam leader of that era. Ulmer attended the conference, which led him to assist the tribe in pursuing the acquisition of a Klallam land base.

The major benefit of the IRA for the Elwha Klallam was federal funding for landless tribal members so that they could regain a self-sustaining community with enough land for farming. Initially, there were no federal funds for the purchase of land. However, by 1937 Indian agency Superintendent O. C. Upchurch was able to obtain federal funding for the purchase of private farms in the lower Elwha valley. The Elwha Klallam acquired 353 acres of trust land at the site of their former village, from which they had been driven out by settlers years earlier (Morrison 1939: 19).

Fourteen homes were included in the purchase. With the assistance of Upchurch, a committee of Klallam leaders selected the fourteen families who were most in need. Many of these families had recently been laid off from their work at the logging camps, and some were living in crowded shanties on Ediz Hook. Through the IRA, the fourteen family heads came together to form the Lower Elwha Valley Association and adopted articles of association and bylaws for an agricultural cooperative. The acquisition of these lands by the Elwha Klallam met with resistance from those who did not want to live on an "Indian reservation" and from sportsmen who anticipated a change in status for sportfishing on the Elwha River (Morrison 1939: 19). Although the purpose of acquiring trust land in 1938 was to establish a reservation, the Elwha Klallam Reservation was not proclaimed until January 19, 1968.

Reservation Community

After the reservation was established, the tribe adopted a tribal constitution and bylaws, thus making available social, health, and other services. Previously, tribal members did not have access to the benefits provided to Indians, such as education. In 1937 Upchurch, who had worked to acquire the Elwha trust lands, wanted to help an Elwha Klallam family that was struggling to eke out a living on a small farm with two young boys suffering from tuberculosis. Upchurch made it possible for the two girls in the family (Adeline Smith and Beatrice Charles) to attend Chemawa Indian School.

After attending school in Port Angeles, where there was considerable prejudice against Indian students, the girls remember Chemawa fondly. Chemawa

Chemawa students Beatrice Charles (third from left, bottom row) and
Adeline Smith (behind her left shoulder). Courtesy of Adeline Smith.

helped the girls to become independent and to realize that they were proud
to be American Indians. Chemawa students were taught to treat each other
as equals, and through their experiences there they learned to get along with
people from different cultures. Although all of the students were American
Indians, they came from throughout the United States and all walks of life.
One of the girls regrets that her mother passed away before she graduated
and she had to leave the school; however, Chemawa prepared her to face the
world without her mother and earn a living on her own (pers. com. with
Jacilee Wray, July 9, 1998).

Since the original 376-acre reservation was created in 1968, growth of the
Elwha community has been slow, because the floodplain prevents certain types
of development. Today the tribe holds 856 acres, 450 within the Elwha Klallam
Reservation and the rest in trust status or fee simple ownership by the tribe.

In 1975 the Elwha Fish Hatchery was built to enhance the fisheries on the
remaining short stretch of river below the dam. The tribal center, which
houses most of the tribe's government business and other programs, was built
in 1976. An intertribal group home, built in 1976, became the site of the Head
Start program in 1990, a tribal health clinic recently opened on Highway 101
west of Port Angeles. The tribe purchased land on the west side of the Elwha

River in 1984 for additional homes, and today there are approximately 412 families living on the reservation. The Army Corps of Engineers built a dike on the east side of the river in 1989, making more land available for housing. Today there are one hundred forty homes on the reservation, but the tribe has 750 enrolled tribal members so there is a need for additional housing.

DAMS ON THE ELWHA RIVER

After U.S. district court judge George Boldt rendered his landmark 1974 decision known as *U.S. v. Washington,* the Klallam regained the fishing rights that are the very core of their culture. But was it too late?

The largest hurdle the Elwha Klallam have had to face is restoration of the Elwha River. Together with Olympic National Park, the U.S. Fish and Wildlife Service, and the Bureau of Reclamation, the Elwha Klallam have worked toward restoration of the Elwha River watershed.

Since 1910 the Elwha Dam has blocked anadromous fish from this majestic and once-prolific river system. Anadromous fish are spawned in freshwater, spend varying amounts of their lives in the ocean, and then return to their river of origin. Although state law required fish ladders when the dam was built, the Elwha Dam project owner, Thomas Aldwell, was able to thwart the law. The fish commissioner had written to Aldwell, saying, "It is out of the question for us to allow another run to beat its brains out against that dam," and pressured Aldwell to build a hatchery. It was not considered legal to have a hatchery in lieu of a fish ladder at the time, but the law was later adjusted to accommodate the Elwha Dam (Brown 1990: 71).

When the hatchery was finally established, it was short-lived. Tribal members recall watching the salmon below the dam batter themselves trying to get upstream. Some ninety years later, the dams continue to block more than 90 percent of the anadromous fish spawning and rearing habitat in the Elwha River. Amazingly, chinook salmon still come to the barrier dam in an attempt to get upriver. Restoration of the river will provide salmon with the opportunity to return to their native river system and allow the interdependent system of life that depends on the salmon, including the culture of the Klallam people, to rebuild itself.

The Elwha Klallam are justifiably wary of the safety of the dam, as they experienced a blowout of the dam in 1912. At that time, the dam was nearly complete; however, its foundation was not tied into bedrock and the eighty-foot dam ruptured. The only warning the Klallam families who were sitting down to dinner had was the barking of their dogs at the roar of water and breaking tree trunks. Elders today recall stories of heading for higher ground on the railroad trestle above the river and afterward seeing

Glines Canyon Dam under construction on the Elwha River. Daishowa
Collection, Olympic National Park.

dead fish in the branches of the trees. Luckily, no one was injured in the disaster, but the cost in Klallam property and peace of mind was immeasurable. If such a catastrophe occurred today, the effects would be much more devastating.

Restoration of the Elwha River is a complex and difficult task, requiring coordination, partnership, and determination. With dam removal, the number of salmon that return to the river could reach 392,000, compared to the 3,000 to 4,000 that returned to the dam site in 1998. The total cost of the project, including acquisition, was $135 million (in April 1999). However, Endangered Species Act listings of Elwha River Chinook and bull trout and changes in water quality standards promulgated by the Washington Department of Health will likely result in increased fisheries and water quality mitigation costs. Dam removal costs are a small price to pay for the long-term benefits. The cycle of the salmon links rivers, communities, and livelihoods together. In a 1998 *Peninsula Daily News* article, Interior Secretary Bruce Babbitt spoke of the vulnerability of the dams and changing values: "Dams are not like the pyramids of Egypt. They do not stand for eternity. We find over the years there are different needs and hopefully we will respond to them."

The Elwha Klallam feel sorrow not just for the loss of an economically important resource but also for the loss of a self-sustaining lifestyle and cultural cohesion. The prospect of reclaiming much of the Klallam's lost heritage with restoration of the Elwha River has energized the tribe to regain traditional knowledge. Much of this work is dependent on the time and dedication of tribal elders working with the younger generation to achieve a better future.

Removal of the two dams will return fishery resources retained by the Klallam under the terms of the Treaty of Point No Point. Restoration of the fisheries will have major beneficial effects on tribal employment, income, and health. Removal will also restore access to culturally sensitive sites that are vital to the spiritual well-being of the Elwha Klallam people.

On February 29, 2000, a great step was taken toward river restoration when the federal government formally acquired the dams for $29.5 million. The Northwest Indian Fisheries Commission stated: "With the transfer of these dams, we have crossed the divide which will lead to the restoration of these salmon and steelhead runs" and the return of the "biological heart" of Olympic National Park (NWIFC 1999–2000: 4). Removal of the dams is expected to begin by 2004, after finalization of engineering details and construction of water quality protection facilities.

Over the next one hundred years, the restored Elwha River system will provide revenues in local jobs, increased tourism, and sport, subsistence, and commercial fisheries, as well as the priceless opportunity to appreciate and understand the interdependence of the environment in which we live.

Heritage Programs

In 1989 Washington State was preparing to celebrate its Centennial, and in commemoration the Centennial Accord was signed between the state and tribal governments to recognize tribal sovereignty. The coastal tribes celebrated this event by reviving their canoe culture. Each tribe that participated carved a canoe with the help of knowledgeable elders for a journey to Seattle. More than fifteen tribes joined in the Paddle to Seattle, which began at LaPush, Washington. Young and old paddled canoes and stopped at traditional village sites along the way. When they reached Seattle, residents throughout the state celebrated the event at a great cultural gathering.

This trip rekindled the art of canoe carving and taught young people the skills necessary for canoe travel. It also brought various tribes and long lost relatives together for ceremonies and provided renewed respect for knowledge of traditional language, song, and dance. This was just the beginning. Now, each summer a canoe journey takes place that includes more and more tribes. It has been more than ten years since the first Paddle to Seattle, and the positive results of this annual canoe event are most obvious in the strength and knowledge gained by tribal youth.

In 1990 only eight people spoke the Klallam language and fewer were fluent, which prompted the Klallam Language Program. The first five years of the program focused on recording and transcribing the voices and stories of the few elders who knew the language. Timothy Montler, a linguist experienced with the related Saanich language spoken on Vancouver Island, has been working with the Elwha Klallam Tribe to write and teach the Klallam language using a standardized phonetic alphabet. The Elwha Klallam have developed curricula and are working on a Klallam dictionary. Tribal apprentices have learned the language from the elders so that they, in turn, can teach the next generation. Through the Klallam Language Program, courses are also taught at the Jamestown and Port Gamble S'Klallam Reservations. Klallam youth use words in their own language, and people are able to once again make speeches in Klallam at community events. Although the language was in a fragile state, the tribe is determined to keep it a living language.

In October 1998 the Elwha Klallam Tribe received an Administration for Native Americans grant from the Department of Health and Human Services to integrate the Klallam language into the local Port Angeles school district programs. The cultural program provides a comprehensive curriculum of Klallam language and culture at Port Angeles schools. After years of struggling to convey the diversity of our community, this program enhances cultural awareness and an understanding of local history, especially that of the tribes of the area. It also instills a sense of pride and belonging for tribal students in the elementary , middle, and high schools. This program is also being taught in reservation language classes after school, at summer cultural programs, and at Head Start. The larger goal is to achieve appreciation for diversity and diminish stereotypes, especially among the youth.

Visitor Opportunities

Visitors to the Elwha Klallam Reservation can tour the tribal center to learn about the tribe's various programs and visit the tribal fish hatchery. It is best to call in advance to make tour arrangements. Access to the beach on the reservation is closed at the present time but may be reopened under a permit system in the future.

The tribe plans to build a longhouse cultural center, museum, and gift shop, where tribal culture and history can be shared and artists of basketry, carving, and beading can demonstrate their skills. With Elwha River restoration on the horizon, the tribe has a great opportunity to work with other agencies to interpret the ecosystem of the Elwha River at a visitor center.

Tim Pysht, a Klallam elder who was born in the early 1800s and lived to be the age of one hundred, made this prophecy: "The Klallam people will almost disappear, but they will come back and once again be a strong people." The tenacity and will to survive has made his prophecy a reality. The Klallam have managed to stand on the land of their ancestors while maintaining traditional values and knowledge. As one tribal elder stated:

> Our Creator gave us this fish to live on and we cherished it, and we respected it. . . . We didn't waste it; we used every bit of it. . . . I may not see the abundance of fish come back in my lifetime, but I would like to see it come back for my grandchildren, my great-grandchildren, and the rest of my people, the generations to come. It was a gift from our creator; it was our culture and heritage. (Beatrice Charles, cited in Olympic National Park, 1998)

NOTES

1. An expression similar to "Ready, set, go!"

SUGGESTED READING

Eells, Myron. [1889] 1971. *The Twana, Chemakum, and Klallam Indians of Washington Territory.* Facsimile ed., Seattle: Shorey Book Store.

Gunther, Erna. 1926. "Analysis of the First Salmon Ceremony." *American Anthropologist* 28(4): 605–17.

Kane, Paul. [1859] 1968. *Wanderings of an Artist Among the Indians of North America from Canada to Vancouver's Island and Oregon through the Hudson's Bay Company's Territory and Back Again.* Rutland, Vt.: Charles E. Tuttle Co.

Kurt Grinnell fishing. Photo by J. F. Housel.

Jamestown S'Klallam

Trina Bridges and Kathy Duncan

*We live with our ancestors in our hearts. Their voices
speak of the trees, the water and all the earth's riches. We
have the foundation of our Indian livelihood, culture,
and spiritual strengths that have existed for centuries.*

Cultural History

The Jamestown S'Klallam lived and prospered for thousands of years on the northern part of the Olympic Peninsula along the Strait of Juan de Fuca. In 1927 Erna Gunther published "Klallam Ethnography," her principal consultants for which were from Jamestown. This work and her field notes contain information about S'Klallam villages at Port Discovery, Port Townsend, and the Dungeness River and a few S'Klallam homes about three miles upriver (Gunther 1924: 23). Her most thorough descriptions are of Washington Harbor, which was still occupied when she was conducting fieldwork from 1924 to 1925. In Klallam, the name of this village is *sxʷčqʷéʔyəy*, which has evolved into Sequim. The Klallam linguist Timothy Montler believes the translation could be "going to the fire," perhaps in reference to canoes traveling toward the fires of the village (Montler, pers. com., January 22, 1998).

Gunther describes duck hunting at Washington Harbor. One method is of particular interest. The hunter places a net in his canoe and hunts at night, making a "pitch fire" in the rear of the canoe. The ducks are caught as they fly into the net from the front of the canoe (Gunther 1927: 205). The implication is that the ducks were lured toward the light of the fire.

In about 1878 there were forty residents in ten houses at Washington Harbor. Gunther does not record the population figure for 1924, but she describes in detail the chief's residence, which she calls a potlatch house:

The potlatch house at Washington Harbor is fifty by two hundred feet in dimension, standing with the long side facing the water. It has a shed roof with the high side [25 feet] facing the shore. . . . The roof is made of planks that overlap. . . . To help support the roof there are three posts in the center of the house. . . . These are about two and one-half feet in diameter, carefully adzed and made of cedar. On the center post is painted a large white circle symbolizing the sun which is the chief's guardian spirit. Such a circle is painted on the front and back of the post, which stands directly opposite the two doors, one on each of the long sides of the house. The posts along the side of the house are painted with bands of red, white and black about one inch wide running about the post.

Outside the house is a series of tall slender posts set about ten feet apart. They are six inches in diameter and painted with alternating stripes of red and white. On top of each post is a small figure of a bird with spread wings. The chief, *Xaɫxé'nim*, who built the house, also carved these figures because the sun, his spirit, told him to do it. (Gunther 1927: 187)

There were three S'Klallam villages around Dungeness, and by 1857 there were thirty-five non-Indian settlers in this area as well (Langness 1984: 262). One S'Klallam family lived on the hill above the town of Dungeness (Gunther 1924: 45). They were told by the settlers to move down to the sand spit (Langness 1984: 263), or Dungeness, according to Gunther (1924: 45). Then they were told to move again, and again, until they were threatened with removal to a reservation.

The Jamestown S'Klallam chief, James Balch, knew of a man who owned property to the east of the Dungeness River and thought the tribe should buy it. Balch and two other S'Klallam men went to see the place, which had recently been purchased for a logging camp. The new owner said they could buy it, if he could continue his logging operation (Gunther 1924: 45). Fifteen S'Klallam families pooled their resources and paid $500 for 210 acres east of the Dungeness River in 1874. The land was surveyed and subdivided, and close to 140 S'Klallam members from Dungeness, Port Discovery, and Washington Harbor moved here (Langness 1984: 264). The community was named Jamestown, after Lord James Balch, but its Klallam name is *nəxʷsƞiyəʔáw̓xʷt̓č*, for the tall firs found here. Some of the original heirs continue to live at the Jamestown community today.

In 1928, four years after the birth of his daughter Harriette, Jacob Hall rafted the large house that had belonged to his father from its original location on Dungeness Spit to Jamestown. Hall added on to the house and was the first person to have hot and cold water, a bathtub, and a lawn mower (Adams 1988; Langness 1984: 277).

The Jamestown S'Klallam wanted a school; however, the treaty only provided for a school at Skokomish. The Jamestown people were persuasive, and in 1878 J. W. Blakeslee was hired to teach the S'Klallam children in a brand-new Jamestown church building (Eells [1886]1972: 207). This was the first church in the county and was also attended by white settlers. Services were held in Klallam, Chinook Jargon, and English (Eells [1886]1972: 205).

This church became an Indian Shaker church in about 1885. The Shaker religion began in the southern Hood Canal region in 1882 and is prominent among all Olympic Peninsula tribes today. (See the Squaxin chapter for the origin of the Shaker religion.)

In 1910 the government built a formal school building for the Jamestown community, and Johnson Williams, a Jamestown S'Klallam, was one of the teachers. Williams had attended school at Jamestown and had gone on to the Cushman Indian School in Tacoma (Langness 1984: 269). In 1921 the government school was closed for financial reasons and the Jamestown S'Klallam students began to attend public school in Sequim (Langness 1984: 271).

Restrictions on traditional S'Klallam practices were enforced through the

Jamestown Shaker Church. Courtesy of North Olympic Library,
Kellogg Collection.

Jamestown School. Courtesy of North Olympic Library, Kellogg Collection.

Indian agents, the public school, and Christian teachings. The Jamestown S'Klallam Shaker church was a gathering place for families and their relatives from around the peninsula. Harris "Brick" Johnson recalled his grandparents telling the children traditional stories until he was eleven years old (in 1923), when the Shaker church discouraged storytelling. The church reasoned that the meanings and morals of many S'Klallam stories were lost in English translation. However, Johnson (1988) noted that "occasionally they might tell 'em in private."

Traditional stories were told to teach the children right from wrong and other lessons of life. One story about a witch named Slapu has many variations. Susie Soloman told it this way to Erna Gunther.

SLAPU STEALS A CHILD

A baby was crying and Slapu came. She had a piece of bark in her hand and she said it was a fish. She stole the baby and took it up the prairie. As she carried the baby a prairie was made every time it cried. The baby was a boy. She kept him a long time and he grew bigger every day. He called Slapu mother and she said, "Don't call me mother, call me wife."

The boy said, "Make me an arrow, wife." She was glad and made him one. He went out and shot a deer. Later he said, "Make me an arrow, mother." She got angry and did not make any. Then the boy ran away and came to Washington Harbor. There was a man, Ts!atsqwehe, who said, "Get into my canoe, your people have just gone around the point." He took the boy over to the spit.

Slapu came and asked the man to take her over. He said, "My canoe leaks." She said she would get some grass to put in the canoe. The man speared a crab. He sang to himself, "How can I get rid of this Slapu?" He told the crab to bite Slapu's feet. Slapu was afraid and moved further up in the front until at last she fell in the water. It still bubbles where she drowned. (Gunther 1925: 151)

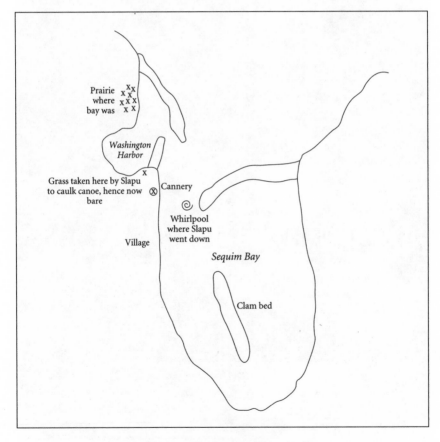

Washington Harbor and Sequim Bay
From a map by Erna Gunther, 1924, University of Washington Libraries, Erna Gunther Papers. Courtesy of Christopher Spier.

Gunther drew a map in her field notes showing where Slapu pulled the grass to caulk the canoe and the place where she drowned. The water at this location continues to bubble today, perhaps from tidal changes on a shoal.

Slapu appears in many S'Klallam stories, and other tribes have a comparable character. She is similar to the witch in Grimm's Hansel and Gretel, as she is always stealing children. The lessons taught by Slapu stories are many.

Jamestown S'Klallam Tribal Center. Photo by J. F. Housel.

Reservation Community

The Jamestown S'Klallam are a relatively small tribe, with 550 members. In 1997 tribal members voted to open enrollment to one-eighth blood quantum as it had been before 1981, which increased enrollment by about 300 members.

Tribal members are dispersed throughout western Washington, but after federal recognition the tribe began to build a stronger tribal government and administration. The tribal reservation in Blyn was officially established on trust land in May 1986 and currently occupies twenty-one acres. This beautiful campus-type facility houses an administrative building, community center, social and health services, and an art gallery. The complex provides a central location and gathering place for tribal services and activities.

Business ventures have been established to provide tribal employment. On nearby tribal property, the tribe operates the 7 Cedars Casino, an economic development office, and a tribal fireworks enterprise. The tribe formed an economic development corporation in 1983 to manage its investments. In coordination with the tribal council, the corporation is responsible for implementing a long-term business plan that reflects the tribe's overall goal of a culturally based self-sufficient community. Tribal ventures include aquaculture, a seafood processing plant, art galleries, art publishing, and commercial real estate.

Tribal committees allow tribal members to be involved in making recommendations to the tribal council. Tribal members are dedicated to serving as volunteers, providing input from the community, and assisting in program planning and implementation.

The five-member Jamestown S'Klallam tribal council guides the community by outlining goals and objectives, developing policy, determining the use of fiscal and natural resources, passing or amending ordinances, and directing tribal programs. Tribal members eighteen years and older can vote and run for council positions. The tribe's government and judicial procedures are outlined in the tribal constitution, which was adopted in 1975.

Between 1935 and 1939, after passage of the IRA, the Jamestown S'Klallam were almost organized as part of a larger S'Klallam Tribe. Because land had already been purchased for the two other S'Klallam tribes, the Jamestown S'Klallam were given the choice of moving to another reservation or staying where they were and remaining unrecognized. They chose the latter rather than give up the land they purchased themselves and lose the independence they had worked so hard to preserve.

In 1953, under the federal government's termination policy, the Jamestown

S'Klallam no longer received federal services provided to Indian tribes. However, the tribe maintained considerable cohesion and was recognized as a distinct community by other S'Klallam groups and other Washington tribes. Characterized as a "progressive" Indian community, tribal members sought new education opportunities and aggressively integrated into the larger community and its economy. A major factor in the stability and continuity of the tribe has consistently been the Jamestown land base purchased in 1874. This provided a geographic center for group identity and independence.

Tribal Status

Although the Jamestown S'Klallam were united as a group by family, language, and proximity and were initially regarded by the federal government as a tribe, they lost that recognition during the termination era of the 1950s because they did not have a reservation, only privately owned land. Without official federal recognition they were denied their fishing and hunting rights. In addition, tribal members were unable to receive health and social services and educational opportunities provided to recognized tribes.

The Jamestown S'Klallam began to seek federal acknowledgment in 1964, but it was not until 1978 that the federal government established seven criteria to evaluate claims for tribal recognition. These criteria were published in the *Federal Register* on December 12, 1980, and are summarized here with specific examples from the Jamestown S'Klallam recognition process.

1. The group must be a specific Indian community from historical times until the present.
2. The group must live in a community viewed as American Indian, distinct from other populations and descended from a specific area. The Jamestown S'Klallam community has existed autonomously since first contact with explorers, and the Jamestown settlement is still occupied by some of the descendants of the original settlers. Others who are not fortunate enough to have that land link have maintained their ties to the Jamestown S'Klallam Tribe through cultural, spiritual, and socioeconomic connections. Although the Jamestown S'Klallam Tribe have many ties to the larger community, they continue to maintain tribal cohesiveness and are considered distinct by the larger community.
3. The group must maintain political influence over its members as an autonomous entity throughout history. The Jamestown community had the leadership of Lord James Balch, and other S'Klallam villages

had similar prestigious spokespeople. The Jamestown elected a tribal chairperson and council around 1910.

4. The group must have a governing document or membership criteria and procedures by which they govern the affairs of their members.
5. Their membership list must be based on descendants from historical times. The Jamestown S'Klallam have a constitution and had a membership criteria of one-fourth-degree Jamestown S'Klallam blood quantum.
6. They cannot be members of any other tribe.
7. They cannot be terminated or previously forbidden federal recognition.

The Jamestown S'Klallam met the seven criteria and regained official federal recognition on February 10, 1981.

Current Issues

Self-determination—the ability to make choices for one's community—has been key to the present and future development of the Jamestown S'Klallam Tribe. Beginning in 1988, seven tribes, including Jamestown, participated in the first tier of the Self-Governance Demonstration Project. Self-governance allows the tribe to set its own budgets, run its own programs, and negotiate directly with the federal government rather than through the BIA. Self-Governance Demonstration Project tribes were added each year until 1994, when twenty-eight tribes officially became self-governance tribes after enactment of the law to make self-governance permanent (P.L. 103-413, October 25, 1994). Up to fifty tribes each year can now obtain self-governance status.

In 1995 the Office of the Inspector General completed an official review of the Self-Governance Demonstration Project to determine whether it was being implemented in accordance with the Indian Self-Determination and Education Assistance Act of 1988. The project was highly praised for its operation and effectiveness. The tribes increased the services they could provide to tribal members for essential programs, such as social services, nutrition, and Head Start. Giving tribes the freedom to redesign and create new programs and establish their own priorities drastically reduced the costs of these programs. In the process, employment opportunities for tribal members increased. Self-governance has led to a "sense of pride and accomplishment because of [the] involvement in the Demonstration Project" (Office of Inspector General 1995).

Self-governance funding supports tribal programs and activities, such as tuition and books for higher education, housing, employment assistance,

Prince of Wales family, shell fishing. Courtesy of North Olympic Library, Kellogg Collection.

family preservation and support activities, water resource planning, and business development. All of the tribe's funding is subject to the federal government's Office of Management and Budget regulations and annual audits.

Self-governance is not new to Indian nations. Tribal self-governance is based on the fundamental principles of tribal sovereignty and the unique government-to-government relationship that exists between Indian tribes and the U.S. government. The Jamestown S'Klallam have emerged as national leaders in this significant victory to strengthen tribal nations' ability to move into the future as progressive, strong, and self-reliant communities.

The sea and rivers have linked the Jamestown S'Klallam to their traditions, values, and beliefs for generations and continue to do so. Many elders still recall childhood stories that include sea creatures such as giant octopus, salmon, and crab. The stories play a large role in maintaining traditional ties to marine resources and continue to influence and guide the tribe in its stewardship of the shell fisheries that they depend on.

The once-bountiful resources of the sea and rivers have laid a path for ongoing efforts to protect and enhance tribal fisheries. The tribe operates oyster aquaculture projects in both the Dungeness and Sequim Bays and is working toward the development of a commercial shellfish business at the local, state, national, and international marketing levels. The Jamestown S'Klallam Tribe places great emphasis on habitat protection, restoration, harvesting, data analysis, environmental monitoring, and regulatory compliance of natural and cultural resources.

The tribe is a member of the Point No Point Treaty Council, a fisheries management consortium formed by signatory tribes to that treaty. The tribe works in collaboration with the treaty council, other tribes, and fisheries management agencies. The Jamestown S'Klallam are self-regulating and have well-established fishing, shell fishing, and hunting regulations for tribal members and an active enforcement agency program.

The Jamestown S'Klallam place great importance on education, family, health, and self-empowerment. Tribal programs focus on physical and mental health in today's society while maintaining tribal identity. The tribe's social services programs include family services, employment, cultural preservation and education, and elder programs, among other preservation and enrichment activities. The tribe is on the cutting edge of health care reform and has one of the first tribally based comprehensive health programs. The Jamestown S'Klallam Tribe works closely with the community to protect human and natural resources for the benefit of all and continues to promote economic, social, and cultural independence so that present and future generations of tribal members can retain their proud and culturally rich history.

Heritage Programs

Meeting tribal members' needs and preserving their heritage is vital to the life of the Jamestown S'Klallam Tribe. Over the years the tribe's cultural preservation and enhancement programs have enabled future generations to value and be proud of their native culture. Today, a core group of tribal members and descendants meet regularly to gather materials for basket weaving, beading, carving, and other traditional activities.

Over the past ten years the tribe has actively maintained an after-school program for teaching S'Klallam arts, values, and traditions. Each summer the tribe presents a cultural program that brings together tribal children from throughout the state to participate in education dedicated to health, social, and cultural activities. The program has grown and prospered into a large traditional event for families.

The Jamestown S'Klallam demonstrate that a balance between traditional and contemporary life can be accomplished and brings many rewards, especially that of becoming a stronger community. As the tribe moves forward to meet the challenges of today, they continue to listen to the voices of the ancestors, "reminding us we are a 'strong people' capable not only of surviving but continuing to grow and provide a positive environment where our children will flourish" (Jamestown S'Klallam Tribe 1998).

S'Klallam language and culture promote tribal identity as a self-sufficient, independent community. All cultures are defined by the words they speak. Loss of the Klallam language would mean losing an understanding of the strength within us. The tribe plans to pursue a grant for a Jamestown S'Klallam language revitalization project, which would build on the work already carried out by the Elwha Klallam Tribe. The project will use existing information and materials to train two language interns to develop additional language enhancement materials and will also involve compilation of spoken histories and the development of a self-directed language work station in partnership with the Northwest Indian College in Bellingham, Washington.

The tribal imperative is simple yet strong. Our language and culture still live in our elders. There is a dedicated effort to ensure that their knowledge is passed among all three S'Klallam tribes and within each tribal community. We must also preserve the physical aspects of our past; the planned museum and cultural center will make it possible to share artifacts, archival material, contemporary cultural items, and photographs for many generations to enjoy.

The Jamestown S'Klallam library is housed in the Social Services Annex at the tribal center. The library collection contains two thousand items, including archival photographs and historical documents. The library is intended to serve as a center for research into American Indian history, culture, art, and contemporary issues. A major portion of the collection contains material on the culture and history of the Jamestown S'Klallam, other tribes, and children's literature reflecting Indian heritage. The library also contains books and journals on American Indian law and policy, health, natural resources, chemical dependency, and traditional arts.

Visitor Opportunities

The Jamestown S'Klallam Tribe proudly owns and operates the Northwest Native Expressions Native Art Gallery, which displays contemporary and traditional art by the foremost Northwest Coast artists. A fine collection of Northwest Coast Native American art is offered for sale, and the history of the art and the artist is available. The galleries support tribal art programs through education and development of new talent. There are two gallery locations. The main shop is located next to the Jamestown S'Klallam Tribal Center at 1033 Old Blyn Highway; another shop is located in the 7 Cedars Casino, five miles east of Sequim on Highway 101.

The 7 Cedars Casino is a beautifully designed reproduction of a traditional longhouse. The tribe received the Cultural Design Tribal Facility Award from the Department of Housing and Urban Development in 1995 for the design of the building. The casino offers slot machines, craps, poker, blackjack, roulette, Keno, pull tabs, bingo, and more. Each evening the Salish Room chefs prepare delicious dinners, including the famous seafood buffet on Fridays. Appetizers and full-service meals are available in the Totem Lounge. The Bingo Bay deli has quick meals and a video arcade for children.

The Dungeness River, originating high in the Gray Wolf watershed of the Olympic Mountains and traveling thirty miles before reaching the Dungeness Bay estuary, is a lifeline for the Jamestown S'Klallam. The Dungeness River Center is a collaborative effort in public stewardship for the Dungeness watershed and its threatened salmon resources. Included in this partnership are the Jamestown S'Klallam Tribe, the Rainshadow Natural Science Foundation, the National Audubon Society, and the Olympic Peninsula Audubon Society. The center is located at Railroad Bridge Park west of Sequim, which is owned by the Jamestown S'Klallam Tribe and managed by the Rainshadow Natural Science Foundation. The foundation board includes a wide variety of community members, the S'Klallam tribal chair, and a tribal staff member.

The purpose of the Dungeness River Center is to enhance public enjoy-

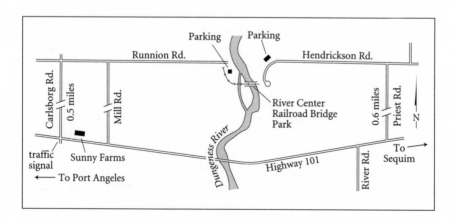

Railroad Bridge Park Area

ment and understanding of important aquatic resources. The tribe hopes that this effort will promote public stewardship of the river and the five threatened and endangered salmon runs found here. Sixty-six species of birds, including bald eagles and five other raptors, have been documented at this site.

The interpretive center features the natural history of the Olympic Peninsula, with particular emphasis on the Dungeness River watershed. The picturesque twenty-five-acre park has an expansive view of the river from the historic railroad bridge. The park includes the Olympic Discovery Trail, gravel loop trails through the woods, a covered picnic shelter, and a seventy-five-seat amphitheater. People hike, picnic, ride bikes, and relax here, and many community members, school groups, and local and state organizations use the park year-round. The trails provide an opportunity for seniors and the mobility-impaired to access one of Washington's most beautiful rivers.

Each September the Dungeness River Festival celebrates the sustainable resources of the Dungeness River. This event, sponsored by the center's partners, the city of Sequim, and various state, federal, and private funding sources, is held at Railroad Bridge Park. There are activities for all ages, including nature crafts, workshops, presentations, walks, storytelling, art activities, education exhibits, and food booths.

Throughout Railroad Bridge Park, leaf prints, river rocks, and sculptured salmon are embedded in concrete surfaces such as pathways, walls, and picnic tables, linking the physical structures with the natural environment. A similar technique is used at the Shellfish Park on Dungeness Bay. An etched tide line and pictures of native shellfish are drawn into the surface of the picnic tables, and interpretive signs nearby explain historic and current S'Klallam shellfish harvesting practices and the future of the shellfish in relation to the quality of bay water. This wonderful picnic site is located at the Dungeness boat ramp near the Jamestown S'Klallam oyster processing house.

The Sequim Bay scenic pullout on Highway 101 in front of the tribal center was developed jointly by the Department of Transportation and the tribe. This site provides educational information about the Sequim Bay ecosystem and a beautifully carved totem pole. Interpretive signs at the site cover local logging history, the lifeways of the Jamestown S'Klallam, and biological information and facts on the estuary and wetland. This site offers printed materials as well. The tribe's dedication to this area is a testament to the continuing resolve of the Jamestown S'Klallam people to protect and respect their homeland.

SUGGESTED READING

Fish, Harriet U. 1983. *Trails, Tracks and Tears*. Port Angeles, Wash.: Privately published.

Keeting, Virginia, ed. 1976. *Dungeness: The Lure of the River*. Port Angeles, Wash.: Sequim Bicentennial Committee and the Daily News.

Lambert, Mary Ann. 1991. *The Seven Brothers of the House of Ste-Tee-Thlum*. Port Orchard, Wash.: Publishers Printing.

Historic Point Julia community. Courtesy of MSCUA, University of
Washington Libraries, UW4971.

Port Gamble S'Klallam

Gina Beckwith, Marie Hebert, and Tallis Woodward

The spirit of the S'Klallam people has been inextricably linked to the land and continues to be the unifying base for a thriving tribal community. The S'Klallam occupied the northern Olympic Peninsula, east of the Hoko River, before the Treaty of Point No Point. When the treaty was signed in 1855, the S'Klallam shared territory at Port Gamble and Port Townsend with the Chemakum and used seasonal sites along Hood Canal (Lane 1977: 2–3).

The Port Gamble S'Klallam had a village on the west side of Port Gamble Bay at Teekalet until 1853, when the lumber mill owners asked them to relocate across the bay to the spit at Point Julia. They build their homes in the style of New England frame houses and were raised aboveground to prevent damage from the frequent seasonal floods. The tribe's community at Point Julia was called Little Boston, a name still used today by tribal members. The small community had boardwalks, a Catholic church, and a schoolhouse.

Dorothy Day George remembers the quaint water system:

> It was sure neat the way the water trough from the creek would flow down and each home had a board they could lift out and get water. It went clear to the end of the spit. In winter we used to eat the icicles. (Port Gamble S'Klallam Tribe 1994: 12)

Lloyd Fulton, another tribal member, recalls the incoming tides at Point Julia:

> I grew up at Point Julia. Our home was at the end of the sand spit and during high winter tides the water would come up even with the floor. (Port Gamble S'Klallam Tribe 1994: 10)

Village near Port Ludlow. Courtesy of North Olympic Library, Kellogg Collection.

Today the community of Port Gamble sits on a west-facing bluff over-looking Port Gamble Bay and the Olympic Mountains.

Cultural History

Before European exploration and settlement forever changed their lifeways, the S'Klallam people had a complex social organization whereby they inter-acted with each other, with other tribes, and with the landscape. They had their own territory, which sometimes overlapped with that of others. The people respected the land and the rich resources it provided, as well as the specific places used by individual tribes. Rather than claim ownership of the animals, the S'Klallam shared the land with them. The balance of people, land, and animals was disrupted in 1850 with the passage of the Oregon Donation Land Act, which offered free land to settlers in the territory that would become the states of Washington and Oregon. The United States offered the land without first obtaining ownership from the tribes. The transfer of ownership from the S'Klallam to the federal government did not occur until the Treaty of Point No Point was ratified by Congress in 1859 (Lane and Lane 1977: 1). Settlers readily took advantage of the opportunity to make land claims under the act.

One of these settlers, Capt. Josiah P. Keller, arrived in Port Gamble with his family and the necessary machinery to start the Puget Sound Mill Company in 1853. Keller worked for a San Francisco firm owned by W. C. Talbot, A. J. Pope, and Charles Foster. Keller found Port Gamble an ideal location for the mill site, with its "large bay, deep water and excellent timber handy to the water's edge" (*Bremerton Sun* 1957: 3). On October 6, 1853, Keller filed a donation claim for three sections of land that included the Point Julia area, the current town of Port Gamble, and the spit at Teekalet Bluff (on the northwest side of Port Gamble).

Keller faced an obstacle to starting his mill at an otherwise ideal location. The S'Klallam occupied the site and their title had not been transferred to the federal government. Port Gamble S'Klallam elder Sammy Charles (b. 1869) described what happened then:

> Boston [white people] are located just about on the edge of what was once the Nooksclime's [S'Klallam] grounds. . . . It just happened that the Nooksclime were camped and fishing on the Gamble spit when the Bostons came. There was talk, talk, talk. The Bostons said that they wanted to put a sawmill there, and would the Indians please move to the other side. There were inducements. There would be lumber, free lumber, and all that the Nooksclime needed to build big houses. They could have the trimmings for firewood, fine firewood, and all they wanted. The clincher was the Christmas treat. . . . The Nooksclime didn't know what Christmas was, but it sounded good. (*Seattle Post-Intelligencer* 1947)

Martha John, who was born in 1891, also spoke of the move:

> The Klallams used to live in Port Gamble, where the general store is now, and all around where the cemetery is located. The mill people came along and sent the Indian over across the Bay, on the Spit. They promised to always have jobs for the men and also gave them enough lumber to build a small house for each family. Every winter the spit would be flooded. A lot of the people died. (Port Gamble S'Klallam Tribe 1971-75)

Louise Buttner (b. 1860), Emily Webster (b. 1883), and Cyrus Webster (b. 1890) described the spit at Point Julia in interviews with John Peabody Harrington in 1942. Emily Webster told Harrington,

> The spit downslope of us was the ancient cemetery. . . . [When] the Port Gamble mill was 1st [*sic*] established, a whiteman gathered the bones of the cemetery, piled them and poured coal-oil on. Joe Tom's [mother] used to tell about this. That whiteman plowed part of the flat downslope of us here, planting spuds. (Harrington 1942)

The Point No Point Treaty was signed by representatives of the S'Klallam, Skokomish, and Chemakum Tribes on January 26, 1855. Isaac Stevens signed the treaty on behalf of the United States.

The S'Klallam, Skokomish, and Chemakum ceded or surrendered approx-imately 750,000 acres to the federal government under the treaty but reserved their aboriginal right to fish, hunt, and gather. The federal govern-ment promised the services of a physician, a blacksmith, a carpenter, and a farmer to teach necessary skills, and a school was also to be provided.

There was no money paid for the land, but article 5 of the treaty stated that $60,000 would be expended over a twenty-year period and "applied to the use and benefit of said Indians under the direction of the President of the United States, who may from time to time determine at his discretion upon what beneficial objects to expend the same" (Point No Point Treaty 1855, 12 Stat. 933, January 26, 1855).

The tribes also reserved a tract at the bend of Hood Canal for their exclu-sive use. This became the Skokomish Reservation. The S'Klallam did not want to leave their homeland or their fishing sites and hunting territory; unfortunately, they were forcibly moved to the reservation anyway. With their canoes in tow, rounding "Marrowstone Point, the canoes' occupants,

Treaty plaque. The area was named Point No Point by Charles Wilkes in 1841 when he saw the point disappear and reappear, perhaps with the changing tides. Photo by Jacilee Wray.

looking back at their ancestral homes, could see their village in flames, burning rapidly to the ground—by order of the Great White Father in Washington, D.C." (Lambert 1992: 67).

The S'Klallam described what it was like shortly after the treaty:

> When all was over the people went back to their villages. The idea that they
> could seek food where they pleased was the theory the Clallams carried away
> and clung to from that time on. The present members of the tribe told me that
> they were not correctly understood at the treaty. This much is certain: They
> disdained the [Skokomish] reservation. While on that reservation, now all
> allotted in severalty, I asked particularly if there were any Clallams on the
> reservation. John Hawk named two, Charley Jones and Mrs. David Charley. He
> did not know of any others. As a tribe the Clallams recoiled from the agency
> ideas and sought to maintain themselves in the old way, taking up what they
> wished of the new food, clothing and weapons brought among them by the
> whites.
>
> Here was independence and pride. The field of land and sea was wide and
> wild. (Meany 1905: 6)

Even if the S'Klallam people had agreed to move to the Skokomish
Reservation, the 3,840-acre reserve was not large enough to accommodate
both tribes, and it was too far from the S'Klallam's "usual and accustomed"
fishing "grounds and stations" as guaranteed in the treaty. With the treaty
signed, the rapidly increasing homesteads deprived the S'Klallam of their traditional lands, and they had no land to call their own.

Although Keller's large donation claim was reduced to only the Port
Gamble mill site, Pope and Talbot and other company men acquired title to
all of the land around Port Gamble Bay, including most of the land where
the current Port Gamble S'Klallam Reservation is located. In 1863 the parcel
that eventually became the Port Gamble Reservation was conveyed to Pope
and Talbot by the University of Washington, which held title through a land
grant selection process. Meanwhile, the S'Klallam remained on mill company
land at the spit at Point Julia and worked at the mill across the bay where
they were regarded as "competent workmen"(Coman and Gibbs 1949: 69).
The newcomers had acquired all of the land bordering on Port Gamble Bay
by 1872, before the S'Klallam could obtain land under the Indian Homestead
Acts of 1875 and 1884.

Without a reservation and with the government failing to meet its treaty
obligations, the Port Gamble S'Klallam began to purchase land. On
December 8, 1886, Charley Jones, John Soloman, and Cookhouse Charley
each bought eleven acres fronting the bay near Point Julia. In 1891 Joseph
Anderson received the final certificate on his eighty-acre parcel under the
Indian Homestead Act. Other Port Gamble S'Klallam who purchased land

were George Dan Howell in 1887, Jacob Jones in 1903, and Ed Purser in 1921. More S'Klallam members obtained land through purchase or gift from other S'Klallam. The process of purchasing land and ensuring that it remained with S'Klallam families demonstrates the importance the S'Klallam placed on maintaining residence near Point Julia. Unfortunately, much of this land was lost to county tax foreclosures in the 1930s.

While some S'Klallam were able to obtain land and make homes for themselves, others remained landless. In 1915 Thomas G. Bishop, president of the Northwestern Federation of American Indians, initiated an effort to help landless Indians obtain homes on the Quinault Reservation. In 1919 the commissioner of Indian affairs requested special Indian agent Charles E. Roblin to investigate and report on allotment applications and unenrolled Indians in western Washington. At the end of this investigation, Roblin spoke about the S'Klallam situation:

> Their condition enlists the sympathy of every investigating official who visits them. They refused the offer of allotments of land on the Quinaielt [sic] Indian Reservation, coupled, as it was, with the requirement that they remove to the lands and live on them. They could not live on them. They would starve to death. . . . The Clallams should be provided with homes near the waters of the Straits [sic] of Juan de Fuca and Puget Sound, their ancient habitat, and near the large sawmills and logging camps where they can obtain work. (Roblin 1919)

The three S'Klallam bands decided that accepting allotments at Quinault would not benefit them. The Port Gamble S'Klallam selected Peter Jackson to represent them in retaining their homes. Jackson stated that to go to "a wilderness of stumps and begin over again would put them back 50 years" (Bishop 1915: 29).

When the Indian Reorganization Act became law on June 18, 1934, the secretary of the interior was authorized to acquire lands for tribes and create reservations for those who were without a land base. Many tribes organized and adopted constitutions and bylaws, subject to ratification by vote of tribal members and approval by the secretary of the interior. Under the provisions of the IRA, the federal government began the process of purchasing 1,234 acres from the mill company near Point Julia. A purchase price of $15,000 was agreed on, and three years later, on June 16, 1938, the secretary of the interior issued a proclamation setting aside the lands acquired as a reservation "for the use and benefit of the Port Gamble Band of Clallam Indians" (48 Stat. 984).

After the establishment of the reservation, new homes were built on the bluff overlooking Point Julia and the houses on the spit that had been condemned were burned down. Harry Fulton, Jr., a Port Gamble S'Klallam tribal member, was interviewed in the 1970s and recalled the burning of the houses on the spit:

> The Health Department condemned the homes so there wasn't anything to do but move. They ordered the homes burned because it was a health hazard. The BIA built the homes that we live in now. Some of the older people didn't want to leave the Spit, because it was the only home they knew. They lived there practically all of their lives. . . . They had to make [Mrs. George Adams] come out of her old home. She was sitting in an old chair, while they were packing her stuff out. She was sitting there crying and talking and singing in Indian. (Port Gamble S'Klallam Tribe 1971–75)

Mildred Fulton DeCoteau recalled,

> I must have been about 15 or 16 when they burned down everything on the spit. I remember an old couple sitting there crying, watching their house. . . . They had lived there all their lives, you know. (Port Gamble S'Klallam Tribe 1994: 13)

Point Julia homes burning. Courtesy of Museum of History and Industry.

Although the Port Gamble S'Klallam had waited many years for a reservation, for the elders who had lived at Point Julia for so long, the change was bittersweet. However, now that their lands were firmly established, the Port Gamble S'Klallam adopted a constitution and began the process to receive compensation for their ceded lands through the Indian Claims Commission (ICC). The ICC was created in 1946 to settle disputes between tribes and the federal government regarding inadequate, or as termed in the act, "unconscionable," compensation for cession of tribal lands. After years of proceedings, on May 4, 1977, the S'Klallam received payment for their claims against the United States. After deducting the $15,000 that the federal government had paid for the Port Gamble reservation lands, the United States compensated the S'Klallam tribes in the amount of $327,237 for cession of 438,430 acres. The effect of the judgment was that the tribe paid for its own reservation and received less than $1 per acre for some of the most valuable waterfront real estate in the country. The three S'Klallam bands (Port Gamble, Elwha, and Jamestown) agreed to divide the judgment equally and to manage each share for community purposes such as social services, community facilities, investment, and employment (ICC 1979).

The Port Gamble S'Klallam had waited more than 80 years for a reservation and 122 years for compensation of the lands they ceded. Today the Port Gamble S'Klallam Tribe has a reservation with 100 percent tribal trust status and no individual or outside ownership. Trust status precludes state jurisdiction and has maximized tribal control over their 1,340-acre reservation.

The Port Gamble people have ensured their survival through an exceptional ability to adapt and adjust to changes imposed on them. They have demonstrated sheer willpower and determination to remain together as a community. Knowing that they can take care of themselves, they found the necessary strength in their own culture to refuse to accept allotments on other reservations. Today the S'Klallam maintain tribal traditions that began before the treaty period. S'Klallam people carry a deep sense of cultural pride, which will continue to be a source of strength for the future.

Reservation Community

The governing body of the Port Gamble S'Klallam Tribe is the Community Council, which includes all enrolled adult members. The Community Council has delegated authority to the six-member Business Committee (more commonly referred to as the tribal council) to act on its behalf in most areas of governance. Tribal council members are elected to serve two-year staggered terms. Governed by its constitution and comprehensive code of laws, the tribe exercises inherent sovereign powers in all areas of governance including law enforcement, crimes, traffic violations, family protection, housing, fishing, hunting, land use, and civil matters. The tribe's police department and court enforce tribal laws.

There are approximately nine hundred enrolled Port Gamble S'Klallam tribal members, and most live on the reservation. The tribe employs nearly one hundred twenty tribal members in various programs and services, such as law enforcement, human services, Head Start, natural resources, tribal court, cultural resources, Indian child welfare, and administration. Other tribal members are employed by tribal enterprises, including Little Boston Bingo and the S'Klallam convenience store, or work on special construction projects such as the recently completed sewer system and housing development.

Port Gamble Bay is the last harbor in Kitsap County still open to commercial shellfish harvesting. The tribe works with the Environmental Protection Agency and the Washington Department of Ecology to keep the water from becoming polluted. The tribe and the state began a shellfish enhancement program with oysters in 1990, then added manila clams in 1994, and in 1998 included geoduck (gʷídəq) (Hess 1976). Saltwater storage tanks preserve and hold live shellfish for commercial sale. The tribe has planted millions of manila clams and oysters on their tide land south of Point Julia. A program to manage the treaty-protected commercial geoduck fishery at Hood Canal and the Strait of Juan de Fuca is becoming economically viable. The tribe's hatchery program rears and releases salmon and nurtures them in net pens in the bay before release for tribal and nontribal harvest. The four Point No Point Treaty tribes have recently developed a wildlife program that has set a standard for management and enhancement of deer and elk.

Current Issues

The tribal council has identified education as one of its primary goals for the community. Port Gamble S'Klallam children attend kindergarten through high school off the reservation in North Kitsap district schools. Reservation-based courses leading to the B.A. are offered by Evergreen State College. Before her graduation from this program, Danette "Danno" Ives told an interviewer that she always wanted to go to college but had to work immediately after high school. She became interested in Evergreen State College's reservation-based program when she realized she could earn a college degree in the community where she lived and worked. Danno graduated from the program in 1997 and says, "I have more confidence in myself and abilities. I even overcame my fear of public speaking" (Ives interview). Today Danno is a program administrator for the tribe.

In 1996 the tribe dedicated its new Head Start facility, including expanded day care services and a preschool. Other tribal educational programs include tutoring, grade incentive programs, summer school, GED study support, and testing assistance. The combination of programs helps to provide incentive, support, continued education, and recognition for S'Klallam students of all ages.

The Port Gamble S'Klallam Tribe has designed and operated its own programs since 1992. Because of its status as a Self-Governance tribe, the tribe receives federal funding directly from Congress. Previously, these funds were issued through the Bureau of Indian Affairs and the Indian Health Service. Careful and efficient tribal management of these funds has resulted in savings, allowing the tribe to significantly expand services to its members.

A state-of-the-art dental clinic was opened in the tribe's health center in 1996. It won an award from the Indian Health Service in 1997 for excellence in dental care. Emergency medical services have also been expanded. The tribe now has professional staff on call twenty-four hours a day, including an ambulance and an emergency response team composed of tribal members.

Port Gamble schoolchildren in 1941. Port Gamble S'Klallam Tribe.

Heritage Programs

An epic four-hundred-mile open-ocean canoe journey to Bella Bella, British Columbia, in 1993 revitalized S'Klallam participation in canoe travel at tribal gatherings throughout the Pacific Northwest. Since then the tribe has participated regularly in annual canoe journeys, such as the A-ka-lat Gathering at the Quileute Reservation, the Salmon Homecoming ceremony in Seattle, and the Power Paddle to Puyallup.

To sustain the diversity of plants and herbs traditionally used by the S'Klallam for healing purposes, the tribe has planted a healing garden in front of the health clinic. The garden is a tranquil place for people to visit, sit, and meditate.

An outdoor amphitheater surrounded by the native plant garden is used for community events, including the tribe's annual Environmental Day. Work continues on the construction of a magnificent traditional longhouse that will serve as a cultural and educational center and a community meeting place.

The Port Gamble S'Klallam continue to engage in traditional fishing and hunting practices protected under their 1855 treaty. They also practice traditions and participate in ceremonies similar to those that existed before 1855.

The Port Gamble S'Klallam are very proud of their young adult tribal members, including Tleena Ree Ives, who was named Miss Indian USA of 1997–98. Tleena represents not only the Port Gamble S'Klallam but also all Northwest tribes, as she was the first Miss Indian USA selected from the Northwest in the history of the pageant. Tleena takes a strong stance against alcohol and drug abuse and advocates a healthy lifestyle.

The reward of living in this beautiful place on the bay is the connection one feels with the natural world. The Port Gamble S'Klallam respect and revere their elders and delight in their children and extended families. They also take great pride in their tribe's accomplishments.

Visitor Opportunities

The reservation is located near the town of Kingston, Washington, on the Kitsap Peninsula. Visitors arriving from the Edmonds-Kingston ferry should take State Route 104 heading west from Kingston and turn north onto the Hansville Highway. Proceed about two miles and turn left onto the reservation at Little Boston Road.

The tribe operates a convenience store and gas station, which offer services to travelers and tribal members alike. Little Boston Bingo staff provide a

Pole for exterior of longhouse, 1998. Photo by Marie Hebert.

family atmosphere in which to enjoy electronic and paper games. The café serves home-style food to patrons and visitors.

Little Boston Road, with its commanding views of the Olympic Mountains and Port Gamble Bay, is a favorite route for bicyclists. The Port Gamble S'Klallam Tribal Center is located two miles down Little Boston Road. Inside the tribal center are archival photographs, artifacts, and a large model of a traditional village that is a favorite field trip site for schoolchildren.

The tribe's fish and shellfish hatchery on the beach at historic Point Julia is a good place to learn about natural resource enhancement. There is a picnic shelter on the spit, and bald eagles frequently soar overhead.

The Little Boston Library was built on the reservation in 1974 and serves North Kitsap County. It was the first public library located on an Indian reservation in Washington State. This unique library serves the entire North Kitsap area.

The annual Stan Purser Memorial Pow Wow, sponsored by the Purser family, is held the last Saturday in February. This is an excellent time to enjoy intertribal dancing, native foods, and crafts at the Port Gamble S'Klallam Reservation.

Every year the Port Gamble S'Klallam Tribe sponsors an Environmental Day to educate the public about issues that affect the environment. This event is held the last weekend in July and has a specific theme each year. Well-known guest speakers discuss important natural resource topics. Although the goal of this event is public education, it is also a day for participants to enjoy a seafood lunch and Native American performances. Everyone is welcome.

The site of the Point No Point Treaty signing is located north of the reservation in the town of Hansville. The S'Klallan name for the point is Hádsks, meaning "long nose" (Curtis 1913: 98). Signs direct visitors to the Point No Point lighthouse, where there is a monument to the treaty. Those who visit the site can reflect on that blustery day in January 1855 when one thousand tribal representatives listened to Governor Stevens make promises for their future.

SUGGESTED READING

Gorsline, Jerry. 1992. *Shadows of Our Ancestors: Readings in the History of Klallam-White Relations.* Port Townsend, Wash.: Empty Bowl.

Gunther, Erna. 1927. "Klallam Ethnography." *University of Wisconsin Publications in Anthropology* 1(5): 171–314.

Hirschi, Ron. 1992. *Seya's Song.* Seattle: Sasquatch Books.

Point No Point Lighthouse. Photo by Marie Hebert.

Tsátsalaltsa, Hattie Cush, by Edward S. Curtis, 1910. Courtesy of
MSCUA, University of Washington Libraries, NA309.

Skokomish: Twana Descendants

Skokomish Culture and Art Committee

Cultural History

Members of the Skokomish Tribe are descendants of the Twana people (*tuwa´duxq*),[1] united by culture, language, and a shared territory on the east side of the Olympic Peninsula. The Twana language, *ti´tuwaduqut´sid*, has been classified by linguists as a member of the Central Salish branch of the Salishan language family. Many Twana spoke more than one language (*ut´sid*) because of alliances with other tribes based on marriage, friendship, and trade.

Twana territory encompassed an extensive area of marine water and shoreline, rivers, and estuaries in the Hood Canal watershed and upland and subalpine areas of the Olympic Peninsula's eastern slopes to the crest of the Olympic Mountains. The Skokomish is the largest river in the Hood Canal watershed. It is a powerful force to this day and is composed of three main tributaries flowing from the crest of the Olympic Mountains through glacially carved valleys into Hood Canal. The headwaters of the North Fork of the Skokomish River are in Olympic National Park, while the headwaters of the South Fork are in the Olympic National Forest. The river, the estuary, and the intertidal delta at Hood Canal's Great Bend have provided habitat for a wealth of resources, including the largest runs of anadromous salmon and steelhead in Hood Canal. Until 1930, when the North Fork was diverted from its channel by a hydroelectric dam, most of these fish began their life cycle in the North Fork of the Skokomish River.

The valleys of the North Fork and the South Fork and the main stem of the Skokomish River were home to the Skokomish Twana, or *sqWuqWu´b3sH*, "the people of the river." Skokomish villages were located near important resource areas at the mouth of the Skokomish River on Hood Canal and along the river's main stem and North Fork. Vance Creek flows from the south into the Skokomish River near its forks. The Vance Creek drainage was the home of an upriver Twana community known as the *ct´welq´we'li*.

Twana settlements were located at the northern end of Hood Canal in Dabob Bay and at the Quilcene, Dosewallips, Duckabush, and Hamma Hamma Rivers. Others were located at Lilliwaup and Finch Creeks and at the present town sites of Potlatch and Union. Twana settlements along Hood Canal on the Kitsap Peninsula were located at Seabeck, Big Beef Creek, Anderson Creek, the Dewatto and Tahuya Rivers, and Mission Creek. Twana people from these settlements traveled by canoe and trail up the Skokomish and other westside rivers into the foothills and mountain meadows of the Olympic Peninsula, where they picked berries and hunted elk, bear, marmot, and other game. Tribal elders have recalled travel in the 1890s and early 1900s by foot and horseback into the high country behind Mount Ellinor and Mount Washington to hunt elk and gather bear grass.

All of the birds, fish, mammals, and plants living in the riparian corridor and the shellfish, fish, mammals, plants, and birds along the tidal flats and in the waters of Hood Canal are revered by the Skokomish for the contributions they make to the Skokomish way of life. Recently, a gathering was planned to take elders to visit Lilliwaup Falls. Sadly, the gathering had to be canceled because the property owner objected. Helen Rudy, a ninety-two-year-old tribal elder said, "That's where my family went on picnics. We used to hike up to the upper falls as late as the 1920's. . . . Why did they do that?"

People who have lived in their homeland for thousands of years have legends that recount events far back into the past. One of the Twana legends is the Great Flood story. Skokomish tribal member Frank Allen recounted a version of the story to the anthropologist William W. Elmendorf in the 1930s: "The Skokomish people had a flood. My grandfather said about eight or nine generations before his time. The Skokomish all put food and their belongings in canoes and then the rains and the waters began to rise. They rose and rose until the mountains were covered. All except one back of *e´lo´at*, [Mount Ellinor] called *dux^wx^we´k^w´adəbətəbad*, 'Where You Tie Yourself.' Just the top of this mountain was showing" (Elmendorf 1961b: 133–34).

Other Twana legends reflect traditional appreciation for plants and animals. Spring salmon and berries given by *du´kWibahL* (world changer) to the people of Hood Canal continue to be treasured resources. The following account identifies a physical feature associated with the footsteps of this world changer.

> There was a man travelling through this country. . . . There is a place where you could see the tracks of this man in the rock; those tracks are washing away now. They are at *da´ša´d*, near Hoodsport. Big tracks just like a man's foot, only longer. This man was *du´k^wibat*. He could make anything, and he changed the world. Up here in the mountains is a place where he sat down and made whales and other animals and you can still see them there. At *e´lo´at*, at Mt.

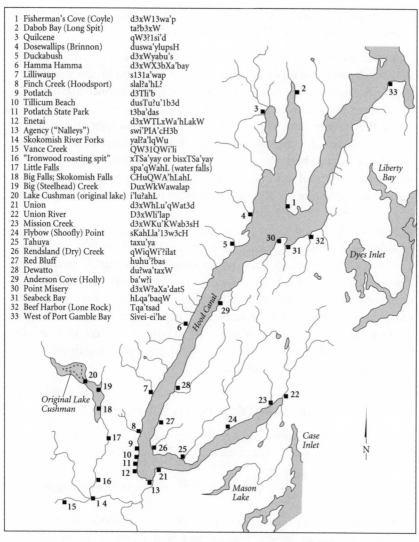

1	Fisherman's Cove (Coyle)	d3xW13wa'p
2	Dabob Bay (Long Spit)	ta?b3xW
3	Quilcene	qW3?1si'd
4	Dosewallips (Brinnon)	duswa'ylupsH
5	Duckabush	d3xWyabu's
6	Hamma Hamma	d3xWX3bXa'bay
7	Lilliwaup	s131a'wap
8	Finch Creek (Hoodsport)	slal?a'hL?
9	Potlatch	d3Tli'b
10	Tillicum Beach	dusTu?u'1b3d
11	Potlatch State Park	t3ba'das
12	Enetai	d3xWTLxWa'hLakW
13	Agency ("Nalleys")	swi'PIA'cH3b
14	Skokomish River Forks	yal?a'lqWu
15	Vance Creek	QW31QWi'li
16	"Ironwood roasting spit"	xTSa'yay or bisxTSa'yay
17	Little Falls	spa'qWahL (water falls)
18	Big Falls; Skokomish Falls	CHuQWA'hLahL
19	Big (Steelhead) Creek	DuxWkWawalap
20	Lake Cushman (original lake)	i'lu?ahL
21	Union	d3xWhLu'qWat3d
22	Union River	D3xWli'lap
23	Mission Creek	d3xWKu'kWab3sH
24	Flybow (Shoofly) Point	sKahLla'13w3cH
25	Tahuya	taxu'ya
26	Rendsland (Dry) Creek	qWiqWi'?ilat
27	Red Bluff	huhu'?bas
28	Dewatto	du?wa'taxW
29	Anderson Cove (Holly)	ba'w?i
30	Point Misery	d3xW?aXa'datS
31	Seabeck Bay	hLqa'baqW
32	Beef Harbor (Lone Rock)	Tqa'tsad
33	West of Port Gamble Bay	Sivei-ei'he

Selected Twana Settlement Sites and Resource Locations Identified
by Skokomish Elders
(*Duwamish et al. v. U.S.A.* 1927; Elmendorf 1992; Swindell 1942; Thompson 1979)

Skokomish, he piled them up. Small rock animals they are, small about the size
of your hand.

The story continues, describing *du´kWibahL's* travels to the different people,
giving them food and teaching them things and doing miracles.

He gave the Skokomish people lots of berries. And he gave them *qʷi´a´tšad*
(spring salmon). . . . You Skokomish, you will have lakes and streams full of

beaver and otter and mink. I'm giving that to you for your dress, to wear beaver skins, otter skins. (Elmendorf 1961: 23, 26)

A prominent physical feature in the region, Mount Rainier, appears in a Skokomish story that was told to the historian Edmond Meany when he visited the Skokomish Reservation in 1905. Mount Rainier once lived on Hood Canal near Quilcene, where she and Mount Constance shared one husband whom they fought over. One day Mount Rainier had enough and left her home. As she traveled over the Skokomish River, she dropped some fish and that is why salmon began to run up the Skokomish River (Meany 1905: 6). In another account of this event, Mount Rainier dropped humpback and silver salmon, reflecting the abundance of these two species in the Skokomish River in the early 1900s (Eells 1892: 28).

Acquisition of food through hunting, fishing, and gathering was part of a complex culture that emphasized the concept that all of life is interrelated. The Twana, like their neighbors, did not view humans apart from their environment or the spiritual world isolated from everyday life. The guardian spirit concept was an important expression of Twana lifeways and provided a foundation for most Twana activities. The Skokomish and other Twana went on quests for their guardian spirits to powerful places such as lakes, waterfalls, and talus slopes in the Olympic Mountains, along the rivers, and in the marine waters of Hood Canal.

THE TREATY OF POINT NO POINT

I do not want to leave the mouth of the River. I do not want to leave my old home; and my burying ground; I am afraid I shall die if I do.

—(S'Hau-at-Seha-uk, To-an-hooch [Twana],

Treaty of Point No Point Negotiations 1855, cited in BIA 1855: roll 5)

At negotiations for the Treaty of Point No Point in 1855, the "S'Klallam, Sko-ko-mish, Too-an-hooch [Twana] and Chem-a-kum" were asked to cede their lands to the U.S. government in exchange for a small reservation at the mouth of the Skokomish River on Hood Canal for their exclusive use. This idea was met with resistance. Twana speakers at the treaty negotiations clearly stated their concern about confinement to a small land base when their existence and livelihood depended on the resources of their entire territory:

> I wish to speak my mind as to selling the land, great Chief: What shall we eat if we do so? Our only food is berries, deer and salmon. Where then shall we find these? I don't want to sign away all my land; take half of it and let us keep the rest. I am afraid that I shall become destitute and perish for want of food.

I don't like the place you have chosen for us to live on. I am not ready to sign the paper. (Che-lan-the-tat, Skokomish, Treaty of Point No Point Negotiations 1855, cited in BIA 1955: 2)

Governor Isaac Stevens and other members of the treaty commission repeatedly assured the Indians that as long as they confined their homes to one area, they would be able to continue to harvest their foods in their traditional places. After two days of deliberations with the treaty commission, the S'Klallam, Chemakum, Skokomish, and other Twana agreed to the terms of the treaty, which included the reservation at Skokomish.

The Twana, S'Klallam, and Chemakum recognized that the reservation at Skokomish would not adequately accommodate all the people, and no one wanted to leave their homelands, fisheries, and family burial grounds. Further, the reservation was far from Twana homes in other parts of Hood Canal and even more distant from Chemakum homelands on the western shores of Admiralty Inlet and S'Klallam homelands along the Strait of Juan de Fuca. The S'Klallam, as a group, did not move to the Skokomish Reservation. The Chemakum, who were few in number at the time of the treaty, were gradually assimilated by their Indian and white neighbors and were counted as S'Klallam by the U.S. government.

Twana from other parts of Hood Canal delayed moving to the reservation as long as possible, but increasing white settlement eventually pressured most of the Twana and Skokomish to move onto the reservation. Some Twana who were able to establish homesteads or acquire other land did not move to the reservation. Shortly after the treaty, Indian agent and former treaty commissioner Michael Simmons recommended the establishment of additional reservations under the Treaty of Point No Point. One reservation was to be located twenty miles north of the Skokomish on Hood Canal where there was good farmland and "an excellent fishing station." Another was proposed for the S'Klallam at Clallam Bay on the Strait of Juan de Fuca (Simmons 1859, 1860). No action was taken on Simmons's recommendations, and the S'Klallam had to wait many years until they had their own reservation lands.

In 1860 the Indian agency for the Point No Point Treaty tribes was located on a large island in the estuary at the mouth of the Skokomish River. This island was a traditional summer settlement for the Skokomish people, where they hosted gatherings for visiting families from other tribes. The Skokomish hunted and netted waterfowl on the island and gathered tule, cattail, and sweetgrass from the estuary for making baskets, mats, clothing, and cordage. Seals were hunted at the north end of the island, and shellfish, herring, flounder, and sole were taken from the tidal flats and deep waters of the bay. Salmon were caught in the salt water by trolling, while in the river large numbers were taken with weirs, by spears, and in basket traps. After the conclusion of the treaty in 1855, Stevens reported to the U.S. government that the treaty commission selected the location of the reservation because of the availability of food resources. As Stevens noted, "[A] considerable stream flows into Hood's Canal near its head—the Skokomish River. There is a large quantity of tide prairie near the mouth of this stream, and it has been selected as an Indian reserve, for it abounds in the food of which the Indians are fond" (Stevens 1855: 260).

With the establishment of a reservation at the mouth of the Skokomish River, the Skokomish Twana were able to remain in a very small but important part of their traditional homeland. In 1882 the Indian agency was consolidated with the Tulalip and Puyallup Agencies and the Skokomish agent was moved to Puyallup. A boarding school had been built on the agency grounds in the 1870s and continued to operate until 1896. Most of the students were from the Skokomish Reservation, and some of the teachers and employees were Twana Indians.

In 1929 Marcus Nalley, founder of Nalley Foods, began acquiring Indian allotments on the island at the mouth of the river for a private gun club and hobby farm. By 1938 Nalley had diked the perimeter of the island, which enabled him to turn hundreds of acres of tide prairie into farmland. Unfortunately, the dikes sealed off sloughs in the estuary and severely disrupted the intricate food chain that benefits young salmon and other marine life. The city of Tacoma later purchased the lands Nalley had acquired. In 1994 a seawall and the perimeter dike were breached by high water. Since that time the tribe's natural resource department has conducted resource inventories and groundwater surveys to document and assess the ever-changing environment that affects tribal resources. The natural resource program also monitors invasive plants like spartina grass on the former Nalley Ranch. Volunteers from the Audubon Society assist the tribe in tracking migratory and resident waterfowl, both on the island and in nearby areas.

Until the 1930s Twana women from the Skokomish Reservation harvested sweetgrass (*Scripus americanus*) from the estuary for making baskets and other items. Industrial and agricultural development in western Washington estuaries has all but eliminated sweetgrass, and only a few remnants of the Skokomish sweetgrass were found outside of the Nalley dikes by the 1970s. In 1996 the tribe began an effort to restore sweetgrass to the tidal area. In cooperation with the U.S. Fish and Wildlife Service, small plugs of sweetgrass were collected from other areas and transplanted in the Skokomish estuary and at the Wetlands Center in the Union River estuary near Belfair. The success of the transplants is still in doubt. Although the sweetgrass plugs that were transplanted in the Skokomish estuary have not fared well, some rem-

Schoolchildren, Skokomish Agency, 1893. Courtesy of Myron Eells
Collection, Whitman College, Walla Walla, Wash.

nants of the native plants still exist here. It is hoped that recent dike breaches
on the former Nalley land will produce the conditions necessary for the
sweetgrass to regenerate to a point where the grass can once again be harvested by Skokomish basket makers.

The arrival of early settlers and the cession or loss of lands under the
treaty brought tremendous change to the Twana people and their way of life;
however, the Twana and their descendants, the present-day Skokomish Tribe,
continue to meet the challenge of these changes. As economic patterns
changed in the late 1800s, many Skokomish became skilled workers in the
timber industry as loggers and mill workers. Some men operated their own
logging companies and small mills, while others took part in the building of
county and state roads and highways. Most families practiced small-scale
farming or had gardens but also continued traditional fishing, hunting, and
gathering activities. Changes in economic activities also resulted in new
meeting places for friends and neighbors who lived on other reservations or
in homestead communities. Indian families from all over the Northwest met
and socialized while working in the hop and berry fields; in later years
reunions and social gatherings began to center around new forms of intertribal activities, such as baseball and basketball.

In 1871 the American Missionary Association nominated Edwin Eells

Indian agent at the Skokomish Agency for the Point No Point Treaty tribes, and the U.S. Indian Office approved his nomination. In 1874 the American Missionary Association assigned Edwin's brother, Myron Eells, a Congregationalist minister, to the Skokomish Agency. Both Eells, the Indian agent, and his brother, the minister, carried out the government's prohibitions against traditional spiritual beliefs and practices, and for many years these practices went underground.

In 1882 the Shaker church, which incorporated both traditional and Christian religious components, became an important part of the spiritual and social life of many Skokomish people. In the late 1960s the traditional "smokehouse religion" that had been banned by the missionaries and the government began a revival in western Washington that was strengthened with the passage of the American Indian Religious Freedom Act in 1978. At Skokomish the traditional religion is known as the Seowin Society.

The Skokomish are determined to carry their traditional practices and wisdom into the future. This determination has been demonstrated in the lives of many Skokomish individuals, such as George Adams, the son of a Skokomish family from the North Fork of the Skokomish River and the first Native American legislator in the Washington State House of Representatives. In addition, Adams was a fisherman, logger, cattleman, and horse breeder. He was a tireless advocate for treaty rights and had great pride in tradition. At the same time, Adams urged his family and his people to become educated in and knowledgeable about the new ways. In 1951 Adams emphasized these beliefs when he addressed a convention of the National Congress of American Indians (NCAI) in St. Paul, Minnesota:

> The 370 Treaties which we were compelled to sign and ratify are your tribal and legal inheritance. They represent the blood, the tears and the lives of your many ancestors; they are the promissory notes of a great and strong nation. The substance of a people say those treaties were for the good of all mankind, and—as long as the waters flow and the grass grows, and as long as the sun rises in the east and sets in the west—we were promised their substance shall remain inviolate.
>
> To you, our sons and daughters, our descendants of a great and noble race, we say that in a few short years you have traveled a long, hard and confused road alone; you are now nearing the end of life's complex trail; you are embarking upon the climax of the claims of the many treaties. Guard them and protect the substances of their many provisions, seek ye the manifestations of their abundant fruit. This is your opportunity—your hour of triumph—to anticipate and acquire the rightful share of your inheritance. (Adams 1951)

Since the signing of the treaty, the Skokomish have made choices and changes in the face of often-overwhelming obstacles. Today descendants of treaty signatories attend college and teach in secondary schools and colleges.

They are involved in tribal, state, and local government. Many are employed in private business or have left the area to find work, but they remain in touch with friends and family on the reservation. The ability to stay on the reservation is governed by available housing. Since the 1970s eighty-four tribal houses have been built using Housing and Urban Development (HUD) funds, with an additional ten funded through the Housing Improvement Program (HIP). Tribal members who remain here carry on their ancient fisheries and work to protect the resource for the future through tribal fisheries programs or teach traditional knowledge and skills to young people. Bruce Miller, a Skokomish traditional leader, explains:

> In the early days of my grandfather, there was an ancient law. It was "*stuxWa?scH3la*," keep the knowledge and memories of our ancestors alive. If a person did not do this they would become "*xwo*" (poor, destitute, have no past or identity, an orphan), they would be a "nobody." They would be unable to have a "*shoyElus*" (guardian spirit board). They would have no foundation in their lives. They would have to borrow someone else's identity, that is to say, become a shadow of someone else's culture. This was truly a sad state of affairs for a people to endure for they would have no resiliency. (Cited in Skokomish Tribe 1991: 14)

The priorities of the Skokomish Tribe today are protection of the marine, freshwater, and land resources of Hood Canal that are the backbone of

Skokomish tribal members Arthur Gouley and Thomas Strong harvesting clams. Photo by Doug Williams, courtesy of Northwest Indian Fisheries Commission.

Twana economy and spiritual beliefs. The heritage of the descendants of the Twana people is reflected in the continuing involvement of the Skokomish Tribe in issues related to the Hood Canal watershed and the Skokomish River, the heart of the tribe's culture.

DAMS ON THE SKOKOMISH RIVER

We are surrounded by examples of how not to manage our natural resources.
—Joseph Pavel, Skokomish Tribal Council, 1991

It is the opinion of all our Indians, that if the whites should offer them ever so many millions of dollars for their land, they would not accept it, because we wish to stay here, and die here.
—Big John, great-great-grandfather of Joseph Pavel, Skokomish subchief at council with Commissioner F. R. Brunot, September 4, 1871

One of the most profound impacts on the Skokomish Tribe, and one of the tribe's greatest burdens, was the development of hydroelectric power on the North Fork of the Skokomish River. At the time of the treaty, the Skokomish Twana had lived in the North Fork valley for untold generations. Legends told that the North Fork was where the Skokomish canoes landed in safety after the Great Flood and where the ancestors of the Skokomish made their first homes. Tribal fishermen knew that the North Fork was the main producer of the largest runs of anadromous fish and steelhead in Twana territory. For many years after the Skokomish and other Twana moved to the reservation, they continued to travel to the North Fork for fishing, hunting, gathering, and visiting. The North Fork was one of the few areas of traditional use that remained free of development and a place of economic, social, and spiritual importance.

In 1924 the United States issued a license to the city of Tacoma to flood 8.8 acres of U.S. Forest Service land on the upper North Fork for purposes of building a hydroelectric facility. Between 1926 and 1930, the city built two dams, two power plants, and a transmission line on the North Fork and on the Skokomish Reservation. The first and uppermost dam was built without fish ladders and blocked the spring salmon and steelhead from their spawning grounds in the upper North Fork. The second dam completely diverted the North Fork out of the watershed through massive pipes to a power plant on the Skokomish Reservation and into Hood Canal. None of the Cushman Project[2] facilities were included in the project's minor-part license, which was a type ruled "contrary to law" by the Federal Energy Regulatory Commission (Chinook Northwest and Martino and Associates 1998: sec. 3: 15–17).

Diversion of the North Fork destroyed fish runs that relied on the glacial-fed waters and had a severe impact on runs that had spawned in the lower part of the North Fork. The diversion reduced water flow in the main stem of the river by about 40 percent.

The project's main power plant on the Skokomish Reservation was built on fill that destroyed a traditional herring fishery and village location. Transmission lines carrying power to Tacoma were built on a corridor that crossed the Skokomish Reservation fronting Hood Canal. The occupation and use of the Skokomish Reservation by the main power plant and transmission line has never been authorized as required by federal law.

In a few short years this project devastated the treaty-protected fisheries of the Skokomish Tribe:

> From the beginning of our existence our tribe has relied on and prospered on the land. We have always supported our families from the land, the water and the river. To this day the majority of Skokomish men support their families by fishing, shell fishing and hunting. . . . Our coho fisheries were shut down this year, as well as our chinook fisheries, and we all know why. Essential water, which nurtures and rears these and other species, has been utilized for other interests, particularly big money interests. Now our tribe is still being prosecuted and condemned for wanting what was promised to us by federal treaty. (Serena Gouley, Skokomish tribal member, FERC testimony, February 1, 1996, cited in Skokomish Tribe 1997: 3)

The effects of the project are evident from the headwaters of the North Fork to the main stem of the river and the estuary on the canal. The dams blocked salmon from 84 percent of the North Fork drainage, eliminating salmon runs of great importance to the tribe. The reduced flow in the North Fork does not provide enough water to support the abundant runs of salmon, which the Skokomish people depended on for subsistence. In addition to the destruction of salmon habitat, the reduced flows are unable to move sediment down the river; the main stem river channel has filled, raising its bed by an average of four feet and reducing its bank-full capacity by more than two-thirds. The result is more frequent and severe flooding in the Skokomish valley and on the Skokomish Reservation and degraded conditions in the estuary delta, which are starved of sediment and freshwater. The water table on lands near the Skokomish River has risen to match the elevated riverbed. Higher water tables have caused increased failures in septic systems and the contamination of domestic well water throughout the reservation. Many homes on the reservation have had to be elevated in an attempt to protect them from the increased flooding. Unregulated operation of the hydroelectric project for many decades has impoverished the people of the

Skokomish Tribe. As stated by Gale Longshore, former secretary of the Skokomish tribal council:

> For thousands of years the Skokomish people have depended on the river for their livelihood. It is our umbilical cord, the lifeline to our people. . . . Years ago the tribe lived in balance and harmony with the River. . . . [T]he fish runs were plentiful, enough for all. (Cited in Skokomish Tribe 1977: 1)

The battle to protect the North Fork of the Skokomish River began in 1913 when the United States protested a dam proposed by the city of Seattle (Holt 1913). In 1930 tribal members filed suit to stop Tacoma's diversion of the North Fork. The federal district court ruled that the tribe could not represent itself and could only be represented by the United States. The United States subsequently refused the tribe's requests to bring suit on their behalf and the suit was dismissed.

Since the original minor-part license to flood 8.8 acres of federal land expired in 1974, the tribe has participated in federal licensing proceedings for the Cushman Project. The Federal Energy Regulatory Commission (FERC) issued a license for the previously unlicensed hydroelectric facilities in July

Skokomish tribal member Bert Wilbur fishing in the Skokomish River. Courtesy of *The Sun*, Bremerton, Wash.

Reflection of Skokomish Shaker Church in floodwater, 1996. Courtesy of
Bonnie (James) Graft, *The Sounder*, Skokomish Indian Tribe.

1998. FERC's 1998 Cushman Project license conditions require provision of
fish passage past the dams and restoration of about 28 percent of the original North Fork flow downstream from the lowermost dam, far less than the
84 percent mandated by the Department of the Interior and endorsed by
other federal and state agencies.[3]

FERC's 1998 Cushman Project license conditions are currently being challenged in the federal appeals court by the tribe and federal and state resource
agencies as inadequate to protect the aquatic resources of the Skokomish
River system and the purposes of the Skokomish Indian Reservation and its
use by the tribe.

Reservation Community

The Skokomish Tribe is federally recognized. Its 4,987-acre reservation was
created by the Treaty of Point No Point on January 26, 1855, and enlarged
by executive order on February 25, 1874. The reservation at the mouth of
the Skokomish River is home to more than 500 of the 807 enrolled tribal
members.

The governing body of the tribe is the tribal council, which receives its authority from the general council. All tribal members over the age of eighteen are members of the general council. The tribe has been a self-governance tribe since 1995 and operates a complete health and dental center under the Indian Health Service self-governance program. Tribal administration also conducts planning, public safety, social services, natural resources (fisheries, timber, and wildlife) management, and cultural education.

The Skokomish Tribe belongs to several intertribal organizations that promote communication and cooperation to protect tribal rights and resources. These organizations include the Point No Point Treaty Council, the Northwest Indian Fisheries Commission, the Northwest Intertribal Court System, the South Puget Sound Intertribal Planning Agency, the Southern Puget Sound Intertribal Housing Authority, the Western Washington Indian Employment and Training Program, and the Olympic Peninsula Intertribal Cultural Advisory Committee. Delegates from the Skokomish Tribe also participate in regional organizations that include the Hood Canal Coordinating Council and the Lower Hood Canal Management Committee.

Heritage Programs

Today the ancestry and legends of the Skokomish are woven like baskets
as legacies to be handed down to the children.

—Skokomish Tribe

The heritage of the descendants of the Twana people is reflected in many ways, including art exhibits at the tribal center that portray historic times and traditional practices. Fisheries programs reflect the tribe's desire to protect the native salmon runs and their habitat. Young people serve on the youth council, participate in the Twana Dancers and traditional carved canoe journeys, learn the Twana language, and celebrate graduation from high school with traditional ceremonies and regalia.

The Skokomish Tribe is committed to providing opportunities for members to improve their education and skills. Career counseling and vocational programs are being developed to meet the needs of Indian students. Other Skokomish education programs are Head Start and a pilot project for young students identified as at-risk. Both programs emphasize use of the Twana language and legends in involving children in the history of their people and in developing problem-solving skills. Tribal staff are working to incorporate the concept of extended family in on-reservation and agency social programs through talking circles and by involving elders as mentors for young people. Many of the nation's social and economic ills are also present on the reservation, and programs are being developed to surmount barriers to learning. The tribe has a long history of working with local school districts to incorporate Indian education and cultural programs in the public school curricula that benefit all students. Kindergarten through eighth grade students from the reservation and nearby communities attend school at the Hood Canal School District elementary school located on the Skokomish Reservation. Students in grades nine through twelve travel by bus about twenty miles round trip to the Shelton School District. The Skokomish and Squaxin Island Tribes have a joint parent committee that supervises use of Indian education funds in these schools. In recent years Evergreen State College has offered reservation-based degree programs.

The Skokomish Culture and Art Committee is currently involved in repatriation efforts under the Native American Graves Protection and Repatriation Act (NAGPRA) to return Twana human remains and associated funerary objects to the Skokomish Tribe. The tribe is one of the twenty-six tribes that have been designated as a Tribal Historic Preservation Office (THPO) to take over historic preservation duties that were previously the responsibility of the state. In 1994, Gregg Pavel, archivist for the Skokomish Tribe, and representatives of the Washington State Office of Archaeology and Historic Preservation negotiated the first Memorandum of Agreement between the state and an Indian tribe regarding archaeological resources. Under the terms of this agreement, artifacts recovered from an archaeological site in Twana territory were transferred by the state to the Skokomish Tribe. The archaeological site is on the Union River near Belfair, Washington, at a wetland rehabilitation project administered by the State Department of Wildlife. As a THPO, the Skokomish are a consulting party in such endeavors when they involve historic properties off tribal lands and have full authority to carry out historic preservation on the reservation. Information about the archaeological site and the associated wetlands is available through the Theler Wetlands Center in Belfair.

Visitor Opportunities

Among the tribal enterprises is Twin Totems, a quick-stop store that sells fresh seafood, baked goods, local fruits and vegetables, and specialty items. Twin Totems is located on the Skokomish Reservation, near the junction of Highways 101 and 106. Individual tribal members also operate small businesses on the reservation that include family-operated fish and shellfish enterprises and art and bead shops.

"Seeds of Our Ancestors," a permanent exhibit of Twana art, artifacts, and photographs, is housed in the Skokomish Tribal Center off Highway 106 near the Skokomish River bridge. Exhibits are rotated on a regular basis and feature the work of tribal artists. Narratives on Twana basketry and culture from "Crows Shells," an earlier touring display of Twana basketry, are included in the exhibit.

Classes in the traditional arts are ongoing at the Skokomish Tribal Center. Efforts to preserve the Twana language continue with tribal members of all ages. Preschool and elementary school children and adults are involved in reviving the art of storytelling and preserving the elders' stories of the Southern Puget Salish people. Denny Hurtado, state superintendent of Indian education and chair of the Skokomish tribal council, explains:

> As a sovereign nation, our goal is to protect our culture and our reservation and to become economically self-sufficient. As our forefathers before us made sure that our way of life was protected in the Treaty, we too, need to make sure that future generations will be able to maintain our traditional way of life and our traditional way of thinking. (Skokomish Tribe 1991: 19)

The mission statement of the Skokomish Culture and Art Committee presents the continuation of time in a way that is meaningful to most modern Twana:

The past is our heritage.
The present is our responsibility.
The future is our challenge.

NOTES

1. The phonetic transcription used in this chapter was developed by Nile Thompson and the Twana Language Program committee. A few of the characters are represented by unique symbols, for examples, 3 = ə, W = ʷ, sH = š, and hL = ł. These characters appear in the Key to Pronunciation at the front of this book.
2. The name of the Cushman Project is derived from the English name of the original lake on the North Fork that was flooded by the first dam in 1926. The original lake was named in honor of Orrington Cushman, who worked for Isaac Stevens's treaty commission and witnessed the Treaty of Point No Point.
3. The Department of the Interior's flow prescriptions are endorsed by the National Marine Fisheries Service and the Environmental Protection Agency as necessary to meet the requirements of the Clean Water Act, the Coastal Zone Management Act, and the Endangered Species Act. The functional equivalents of the Interior Department's flow conditions are endorsed by the Washington

State Departments of Ecology and Fish and Wildlife, the Pacific Fisheries Management Council, the Hood Canal Coordinating Council, and Mason County's Skokomish River Flood Plan.

SUGGESTED READING

Elmendorf, William W. 1993. *Twana Narratives: Native Historical Accounts of a Coast Salish Culture.* Seattle: University of Washington Press.

Skokomish Indian Tribe. ca. 1991. *Portrait of a Tribe: An Introduction to the Skokomish Tribe.* Shelton, Wash.: Skokomish Indian Tribe. Copies are available from the Skokomish Tribal Center, N 80 Tribal Center Road, Shelton, WA 98584.

Thompson, Nile, and Carolyn Marr. 1983. *Crow's Shells: Artistic Basketry of Puget Sound.* Prepared for the Skokomish Indian Tribe with support from the Folk Arts Program of the National Endowment for the Arts. Seattle: Dushuyay Publications.

Aerial photo of Squaxin Island and Mount Rainier. Photo by
Theresa Henderson, Squaxin Island Archives.

Squaxin Island

Theresa Henderson, Andi VanderWal, and the Squaxin Island Heritage and Culture Committee

We are the People of the Water,
From the Squawksin (Case Inlet), Steh-Chass (Budd Inlet), Sawamish/
T'Peeksin (Totten Inlet), Squi-Aitl (Eld Inlet), Sa-Heh-Wa-Mish (Hammersley
Inlet), Noo-Seh-Chatl (Henderson Inlet), and S'Hotle-Ma-Mish (Carr Inlet).

Squaxin Island tribal members are direct descendants of the maritime clans that lived and prospered along the shores of the southernmost inlets and surrounding watersheds of Puget Sound for thousands of years. They shared resources as well as language, as the clans all spoke Lushootseed, of the Salishan language family. These groups also had their own places, and geographic boundaries were mutually agreed on.

Stretching between the rugged mountain peaks of the Olympic Peninsula and the snowcapped volcanoes of the Cascades, inlets of ocean water extend southward like fingers on a hand. Within the palm of this hand is the heartbeat of our people, a small island known as Squaxin. This tiny island, shrouded by sea fog and rain and blessed with salmon and cedar, has remained undaunted by the ebb of time. One with the sea that surrounds her, the pulse of the island is rhythmic and primal; it has become the very soul of the tribe whose name it bears.

The people now known as the Squaxin Island Tribe are committed to the honoring of Mother Earth, the resurgence of our traditional ways and the respect and protection of all people, not only those who are living but also those who have gone before and who are yet to be born.

We are a diverse and proud people. Our unity as a tribe goes beyond geography. Once we were many communities with a similar language. Following our confinement on the island, we once again dispersed. We are a returning people, returning to our land, returning to our culture. Our long memories, our ingenious adaptiveness and our confidence in knowing who we are have led to our continuing existence.

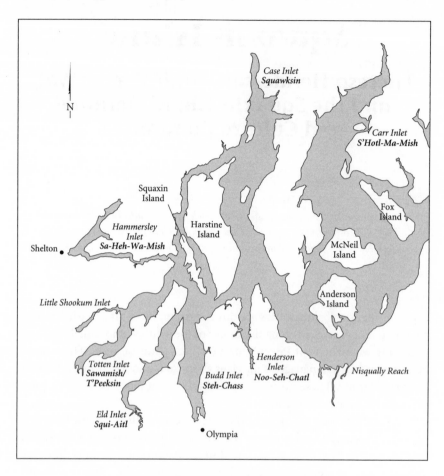

The Seven Inlets of South Puget Sound
Squaxin Island Archives.

Our tribal family seeks to maintain the pride, honor, and dignity that is our traditional way. Through art, singing, ceremonies, fishing, vocations and traditional medicine, we celebrate the individual abilities and talents, which have made us the people we are today. It is our intent that our lives and our work be meaningful and will contribute to the well-being of the entire tribe. We believe this will bring about a resurgence of our culture.

Our greatest natural resource is our elders. They are our history. Another valued resource is the children. They are our future. It is the privilege and the responsibility of the young adults to see to it that the elders and the children are honored and nurtured.

We believe that the Great Spirit is with us in everything we do, and to maintain our relationship to Mother Earth and to achieve physical, mental and spiritual health, we will always need to remember who we are and why we are here. (Squaxin Island Tribe Mission Statement)

Cultural History

Historically, Squaxin Island was a gathering place. Songs sailed out across the waterways as Squaxin Island ancestors paddled their magnificent cedar canoes to the island to trade, attend a family potlatch, or gather from the native cherry tree.

The waterways were the highways, and people traveled extensively along them, as far north as Vancouver Island and out to the Pacific Coast via Black Lake, the Chehalis River, and Grays Harbor to the Columbia River basin. As they traveled by canoe, people listened to the elders tell legends passed down through the generations. Through storytelling, the young ones learned by example.

Archaeological and ethnographic information reveals that there were extensive trade routes throughout the North American continent. The Squaxin Island people traveled in the Northwest on well-established trails across the Cascades into Yakama country, to the Columbia River and far beyond. Many of today's highways were built along existing trail routes, worn deep by centuries of continuous use.

The Squaxin Island people lived in longhouses and slept on pallets of cedar, cattail, or fern. Blankets were woven of mountain goat and dog fur laced with thistle or feather down. These blankets provided more than warmth; they were an indication of great wealth. A particular breed of dog was raised for its fur and kept on small islands from which they could not escape. Captain Vancouver saw wool dogs near Port Orchard that "resembled those of Pomerania," though a little larger (Meany 1907: 136). The Squaxin Island people's spoken history relates that these dogs became extinct by the late 1800s. Hunters also had dogs, which may have been a different breed, to help track prey. Nets were cleverly strung across the inlets to trap ducks, geese, and other birds.

Artwork, clothing, basketry, ropes, eating utensils, bentwood boxes, and canoes were made of cedar. Most items used in villages were made of wood and grass fibers. Both men and women wore woven cedar and sometimes leather. They wore decorated regalia on special occasions and put goose down in their hair and used otter wraps on their braids.

The sea and its salmon runs were highly respected, as were berries, clams, mussels, crab, and other delicacies offered from the heart of the earth. The aquatic creatures that sustained the ancestors and gave them life offered much more than mere physical nourishment; they provided spiritual sustenance as well. Each person had a spirit guide, be it Killer Whale, Frog, Raven, Beaver, Seagull, Flounder, Otter, Eagle, Bear, or Wolf, that protected individuals from evil and guided them through the dangers of the spirit world. These spirits empowered the individual in aspects of daily life. For example, the loon was a great fishing power but also made a man brave and a good hunter. Other types of power provided the individual with the ability to prophesy or heal the sick.

In 1853 the county surrounding the narrow inlet of Big Skookum (a Chinook Jargon term for "strong"), now known as Hammersley Inlet, was named in honor of the Sa-Heh-Wa-Mish people. Sa-Heh-Wa-Mish continued to be the name of the county until 1864, when the name was changed to Mason County.

On Christmas Day in 1854, the Treaty of Medicine Creek was negotiated in Chinook Jargon, a trade language inadequate to convey the complex issues of treaty making. This treaty was signed on December 26 and was the first in Washington Territory. More than 650 people attended the negotiations held at Medicine Creek on the Nisqually Delta, despite the miserable chilling rain.

Of thousands of square miles encompassing the ceded area of the people, only one small island, four and a half miles long and one-half mile wide (1,496 acres), was retained as the area where all of these groups were to reside. The island, previously known as Klah-Che-Min, was given the name of the Squawskin people from Case Inlet and became known as Squaxin Island.

In the Lushootseed language, Squawskin has several interpretations. One meaning is "split apart," as spoken history "recounts that the land here was opened by force, the water entering and making a bay" (Waterman 1920: Squaxin Site No. 1). It has also been known to mean "in between," or "piece of land to cross over to another bay," signifying the location of the village site on the isthmus between Hood Canal and Puget Sound.

The neighboring tribes of Nisqually and Puyallup were also signatories to the Treaty of Medicine Creek. The Indian War of 1856–57 erupted after the tribes became fully aware of the terms of this treaty and fought to secure a more suitable land base. During the war, hundreds of Indian people were confined on Squaxin Island, which became the local Indian agency headquarters in 1857. A blacksmith station, a church, and a school were established soon after (ARCIA 1857).

The Indian agent wanted to make farmers of the Squaxin Island people and tried unsuccessfully to force them to settle down in one place and raise crops. This was not a productive way of life for people used to traveling to harvest the seasonal resources of the sea and the land. When the war ended in 1857, the Squaxin Island people resumed their traditional migratory way of life, harvesting berries, cedar, marsh grass, vegetables, and roots such as

Medicine Creek, site of the first Indian treaty. Photo by Edward S. Curtis, 1914. Courtesy of Washington State Historical Society.

camas and returning to the salmon runs in the fall. In 1859 fifty island residents died of introduced diseases. There was no drinking water available on the island, so it had to be carried by canoe from neighboring Hope Island.

Gradually, the Squaxin Island people began to leave the island to take up permanent residence near their original homes. By 1862 the number of island residents had dwindled to fifty. With so few tribal members remaining on the island, the Indian agency headquarters was moved to Puyallup.

Because of low attendance, the school was moved from Squaxin Island to the Puyallup Reservation, near the mouth of the Puyallup River. Flooding in 1873 led to the removal of the school to higher ground, and it became a boarding school. The school continued to operate with congressional funding until its closure in 1915, when the children attended the newly integrated public school system. Squaxin Island children also attended Chemawa Indian School in Oregon. One family has their great-great-grandfather's book of autographs from fellow Chemawa students dating to 1887.

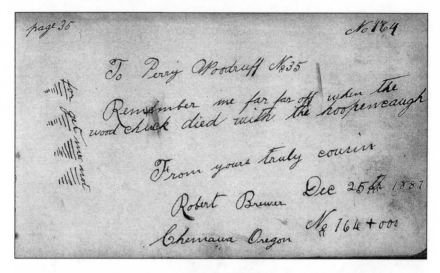

Autograph page. Courtesy of Andi VanderWal.

Historically, some people on the island lived in cedar plank homes. Others lived in float houses, which they pike-poled from one place to another with the tide and moored in sheltered coves. The latter houses provided easy access to their oyster beds but also presented a challenge. One unfortunate resident found himself marooned on Harstine Island after an exceptionally stormy night. Float houses were often stranded on the beach in the summer months and afloat during high winter tides.

Flooding is a common occurrence in western Washington but nothing compared to the Great Flood that deluged the region some time long ago:

> The people were told to prepare several canoes and stock them with enough food supplies for many days, as it was going to rain and there would be a Great Flood. It rained and rained until the water was so deep it was up to the mountaintops. The people took out their ropes and tied their canoes to the top of the Olympic Mountains to keep from drifting away and getting lost.
>
> The rain eventually stopped and the water started to recede. Some of the canoes broke loose and floated away to the north, south, east, and west. The ones that floated south settled in what is now known as the Puget Sound basin, thus creating all the bands that are our ancestors. (Squaxin Island Tribe)

The men worked as loggers, and families worked in the hop and berry fields to make ends meet; however, they continued to harvest salmon, smelt, herring, clams, and oysters, and the women made baskets and cedar dolls for sale in Olympia to collectors and tourists. The somewhat profitable but time-intensive occupation of basket weaving flourished around the turn of the century. Steamer ships drew near to the island each Saturday morning, picking up the Squaxin Island women who stood on the floats loaded with their goods to sell. Saturdays became known as "Indian Day" and were eagerly awaited.

By 1959 there were only four year-round residents on the island. Those who had moved to the mainland often returned for a potlatch with families and friends. They traveled from Arcadia Point to Squaxin Island on rafts with their horses.

In 1899 the state of Washington attempted to lease tidelands on the Squaxin Island Reservation that were owned by the original allottees. Concerned tribal members took the matter to court and in 1903 regained full ownership of the tidelands and control of access to the island.

The Squaxin Island Tribe filed a claim under the Indian Claims Commission Act for compensation for the lands they ceded to the government. The government's settlement of only $7,661.82 in 1974 was based on lands that were occupied only by the "Squawksin Band" at the head of Case Inlet. The commission had mistakenly interpreted the posttreaty term "Squaxin Island Tribe" to mean the same as the treaty term "Squawksin Band." This settlement neglected to provide compensation for the lands of the other six bands, and the Squaxin Island Tribe refused to settle. The funds have remained in a BIA trust account ever since.

Theresa Nason and Nellie Krise on Squaxin Island. Squaxin Island Archives.

SHAKER CHURCH

One of the most well-known aspects of the Squaxin Island Tribe is the motherhood of the Indian Shaker Church. Founded by Squaxin Island tribal member John Slocum in 1882, the church continues to have an active membership throughout the western United States and Canada.

John Slocum was the grandson of Old Chouse, a respected leader of the Sa-Heh-Wa-Mish, known to all Puget Sound Indians. Old Chouse, a firm believer in traditional spiritual practices, died in the 1860s, at the reported age of 100.

In November 1882, at the age of forty, Slocum fell ill while operating his small logging camp at Skookum Inlet (Barnett 1957: 37). In a firsthand account by Annie James, a younger sister of John's wife, Mary, Annie says that John Slocum died from a broken neck in a fall while logging (Barnett 1957: 30). Slocum's father and brother paddled to Olympia for a casket (Gunther 1949: 38); meanwhile, at Slocum's home on Hammersley Inlet, his body began to stir; he sat up and began to speak (Eells [1886] 1972: 264). Two of his brothers "crossed the bay and got a fast horse to go to Olympia and tell his father not to bring the coffin" (Gunther 1949: 39). Slocum claimed that God had sent him back to life with a message for the Indian people to believe in the man named Jesus, whom they had learned about from the Catholic mission established along the eastern shore of Budd Inlet in 1848.

Soon after Slocum's reported resurrection, he and some of his new followers built a cedar and tule mat church at the site. Slocum began to preach at his new church on Church Point, until the August following his "death," when he again fell ill (Gunther 1949: 40). John's wife, Mary, walked to a nearby stream for private prayer and meditation. As she prayed, a tremor came over her and her whole body began to shake. She returned to the house and shook over John's head. Once again he began to stir, and thus Mary became known as the bearer of the power of the shake that is believed to bring healing to those who are physically or spiritually ill.

To this day members of the Shaker church travel great distances to help those in need. The Shaker religion is viewed as a gift sent by Jesus Christ and a way for American Indians to serve him. It spread quickly to surrounding groups; by 1885 it was practiced at Jamestown and other S'Klallam villages. By 1890 it had reached Taholah, then LaPush in 1902, and Neah Bay in 1903 (Amoss 1990: 635). Although some Indian agents and missionaries attempted to suppress the Shaker church, even to the extent of chains and imprisonment (Krise 1940), it gained momentum, because it allowed people to continue worshiping in a traditional way. The Shaker religion was "legally constituted" as a church in 1892 and incorporated under Washington State law in 1910 (Amoss 1990: 633–34).

By the late 1800s Church Point was taken out of the hands of the Slocum family by an executive order of the president and deeded to a ship captain under the Oregon Donation Land Act, and Indian access to the sacred site was restricted. More than one hundred years later, in June 1995, the tribe bought back Church Point and members of the Squaxin Island Tribe and the Shaker church celebrated the reacquisition.

The Squaxin Island Community Today

We continue to be the people of the water. We are of the bays, inlets, and the streams. Our lives depend on the stewardship we extend to all the earth, and the resources given to us as a gift from the Creator.

After years of struggling to retain their language, culture, and livelihood, the People of the Water have endured like a remnant of a tightly woven fabric. As early as 1928 they held meetings to reestablish themselves as a functioning tribal government. After the tribe reorganized in 1965 under provisions of the Indian Reorganization Act, the tribal government and the community itself were reestablished. The tribe purchased lands in the Kamilche area in the 1970s that have continued to develop into a considerable land base. Many of the tribe's 692 tribal members are returning after years of separation. Squaxin Island tribal members remain focused on sustaining and protecting their rich culture, embracing responsibility for natural resources, and nurturing their most valuable assets, the elders and children.

Today there are no year-round residents on Squaxin Island, yet the island is viewed as the bond that unites past, present, and future generations. It is revered for its tragedies, its blessings, and its potential. It is a reminder of who we are in relationship to our ancestors, our natural resources, and ourselves. Squaxin Island is used for fishing, hunting, shellfish gathering, camping, and other cultural activities. Only tribal members are allowed on the island; however, permits can be obtained through the tribe's natural resources department for tribal members to take friends on the island with them.

The general council of the Squaxin Island Tribe elects a seven-person council that oversees all branches of tribal government and enterprise. The tribe was one of the first twenty-eight tribes to enter into the Self-Governance Demonstration Project with the federal government. Now the tribe establishes its own priorities and budgets for funds previously administered by the Bureau of Indian Affairs.

Each year the tribe awards several college scholarships to young tribal members. The children are involved in traditional arts, crafts, and cultural classes, and young dancers perform at public schools, community events, and American Indian ceremonies.

In 1986 young people designed the Squaxin Island logo (below) incorporating family crests. Chum Salmon was chosen for the overall image, because it is he who keeps the Squaxin Island people alive during the long winter months.

All animals are important—no one is greater than another.
All are part of the circle of life.

Chum Salmon—Chum Salmon is the greatest fighter! Legend tells us that when salmon were created, Raven had to swim to the center of the ocean to look for food for people. Chum was the last salmon to come out because he is a strong fighter! The elders say you can catch a Chinook by one tooth, but without the spirit of Chum Salmon, our people would not be alive today. The vitamins and oil he gives us keep us alive and healthy.

Raven—He is the mischievous guardian of the forests and their animals. If you want to know where Elk is, ask Raven. He will tell you!

Killer Whale—He is the symbol of the water, and water is everything. Killer Whale is one of the creatures of the sea that breathes as man. Killer Whale is the wolf of the waters. He is our protector.

Wolf—Wolf teaches us true family harmony. The Wolf leader does nothing without considering the welfare of the entire community, and all members work and play together in perfect unity.

Bear—Bear is the protector of Life (Woman). Because Bear follows all of the Creator's rules, Bear has a close relationship with the Creator. Bear sleeps through the winter and never worries about starving to death. Bear's childbirth takes place while asleep, so Bear never experiences the pain of childbirth.

Beaver—As the keeper of kindness and harmony, Beaver is the builder-worker. While the Indians roamed, Beaver made a sacrifice to stay and protect the valleys. Without his dams flooding the lowlands, there would be no water in the summer. Beaver would rather turn his back than fight anytime!

Frog—Good luck! Having Frog as a spirit helper is good fortune. When Frog stops croaking, you know something is up. Frog was Raven's helper in bringing the sun, moon, stars, water, and man.

Squaxin Island Tribal Cultural Center. Photo by Theresa Henderson,
Squaxin Island Archives.

The cultural center complex consists of three buildings. The first building
to be constructed is the Elder's Center, home to tribal elders' programs as
well as the cultural resources department. Phase 2 of the cultural center complex is the Squaxin Island Museum Library and Research Center. The
museum is an important tribal home for a rare cedar gillnet uncovered at a
large village site in Eld Inlet as well as other cultural items. Phase three of the
cultural center complex is an administration building. The residential area
surrounds the cultural center and other tribal government facilities. The cultural resources department identifies, protects, and preserves the numerous
cultural sites in the ceded territory.

The Squaxin Island people are historic stewards and present-day co-man-
agers of fisheries and other natural resources. The tribe participates in natural resource protection and enhancement with the Northwest Indian
Fisheries Commission, the Puget Sound Water Quality Authority, the
Washington Department of Fish and Wildlife, and other groups and agencies
to ensure that today's decisions provide for a healthy future.

Management decisions are made so as to protect the resources for generations of descendants. The Squaxin Island people believe that salmon people
are their relatives and the salmon's homes must be respected and protected.
The first salmon to return each fall is welcomed and honored in a sacred ceremony. The salmon are linked with immortality, eternity, and rebirth. As

characterized by the Squaxin Island Tribe, "*Salmon run not only in the ocean and streams; their spirit runs through our blood and in our souls.*"

The tribe's first salmon story follows:

THE FIRST SALMON

Once there was a little boy and he loved salmon. He played with the salmon and he swam with the salmon. Finally the salmon people decided to take him home with them. He wanted to go, so they took him to where the salmon people live. He lived there for several months or maybe even years. The boy began to get homesick, so the salmon people agreed to take the boy back to visit his family. The salmon people knew they were going for two reasons—to bring the little boy back and to bring food to his family.

Messages were sent so the family would know what time of year the salmon people were coming. And so they prepared real carefully, cleaning the streams and cleaning the beaches, preparing for the salmon boy and the salmon people to come. The family had the ferns and the moss ready and waiting. And they caught the first salmon, cleaned him carefully, made sure everything was taken care of, and then cooked him. But before they cooked the salmon, they took the skeleton, very carefully and very ceremoniously, back down to the beach. They placed the skeleton upstream to show the direction for the rest of the salmon people who were bringing the boy back for a visit. The message was clear; the family of the boy was taking very good care of the salmon that were coming back.

Every year they still come back to visit, and it is very important for us to make sure that they are welcome, taken care of, and everything is waiting for them, including clean beaches and streams.

The Squaxin Island Tribe, in cooperation with the State Department of Fish and Wildlife, operates one of the largest tribal coho salmon saltwater net-pen enhancement programs in the Northwest. The net-pen facility is located between Squaxin and Harstine Islands in Peale Passage. These net-pens are floating structures 300 feet long by 62 feet wide. They are divided in half by a walkway, with ten 25-square-foot openings on each side. Within each opening is a nylon net that extends 12 feet deep, with attached weights to keep the nets from billowing or collapsing in tidal currents, creating large underwater cages in which to raise the young fish. The pens are covered with netting to protect the young salmon from predators, such as birds and otters.

The three- to four-inch salmon are transferred from nearby freshwater hatcheries to the seawater net-pens in January each year. At the hatchery they are put into large tanker trucks and driven to the dock. At the dock the fish are transferred through pipes into two 1,500-gallon water tanks mounted on a barge. Each tank has a carrying capacity of fifty thousand fish. Fresh salt water is circulated in the tanks during transport. The barge is then pushed to the net-pens by a small tugboat, and the fish are transferred into the waiting net-pens.

The small salmon eat fish food until the end of May, when they reach six or seven inches, and are released into Puget Sound for their migration out to sea. Physiological changes occur when the salmon migrate from freshwater to the sea, during the smolt period. Up to 2.5 million coho salmon are released from these pens. In one year, the salmon that return from their migration will provide fish for commercial and sportfishing throughout Puget Sound.

Clams and oysters are part of the tribe's culture and survival. The Harstine Oyster Company was acquired in 1976, along with 2,300 feet of tideland frontage, which is planted with oysters every year. The business employs approximately twenty people during the summer months. In addition to processing Pacific oysters, the company rears mussels. Tribal members harvest clams and geoduck under tribal permits on traditional tidelands and in deep water.

Harstine Oyster Company barge. Photo by Theresa Henderson, Squaxin Island Archives.

Visitor Opportunities

The tribal center is located on Klah-Che-Min Drive, approximately one mile from the intersection of Highways 101 and 108, off the Old Olympic Highway. The center includes administrative offices and the Tu'Ha Buts Learning Center. The tribal center is open to the public and houses a portion of the tribe's collection of historic photographs, baskets, and other art and artifacts, which will be moved to a new tribal museum scheduled to open in spring 2002. When complete, the Squaxin Island Museum Library and Research Center, named k^wədig^wsʔaltx^w (home of sacred belongings), will provide a gathering place for generations of Squaxin Island people and a symbol of pride and identity for the community. k^wədig^wsʔaltx^w will be a repository for the care and preservation of traditional artforms and an archive to protect historical documents and photographs. Artifacts recovered from the archaeological site at Mud Bay will be featured in the museum, along with other exhibits that depict the living culture and traditions of the people of the water.

The Kamilche Trading Post, a retail shop that offers Native American handicrafts, quick-stop groceries, gas, and fresh Harstine Oyster Company seafood, is located at the intersection of Highways 101 and 108. All enterprises are tribally owned, including summer fireworks sales at the store. The tribe uses proceeds from the sale of fireworks to provide for social programs and law enforcement.

In 1862 the Indian agent at Squaxin Island, W. B. Gosnell, noted that the people would "not quit gambling," because the urge to acquire riches through games of chance were ever present among the Squaxin Island people. Horse racing and bone game celebrations were also an important part of the culture. These games could last through the night and were serious business. People entered into them with determination to win, and large groups participated as spectators, placing bets (ARCIA 1862).

Early on the state of Washington suppressed nearly all gaming operations among the Squaxin Island people, leaving only bingo. In the mid-1980s the Cabezon Tribe of California successfully affirmed in court that the state does not have jurisdiction over their sovereign tribal government and their gaming operations. California and many other states petitioned Congress to intervene, and the Indian Gaming Regulatory Act was instituted in 1988. This act addresses classification, authorization, location, and jurisdiction of tribal gaming facilities. The state of Washington signed a gaming compact with the Squaxin Island Tribe on January 26, 1995; however, electronic gaming devices were disputed between the parties. In 1997 a federal court ordered the parties to negotiate, and an agreement was reached for a tribal lottery system to be modeled after the state lottery, played with electronic equipment called video lottery terminals.

Little Creek Casino opened in September 1995. With a staff of several

kʷədigʷsʔaltxʷ, Squaxin Island Museum Library and Research Center. The newly constructed museum's facade represents Thunderbird. Courtesy of Schacht I Aslani Architects.

hundred, it is one of the largest employers in Mason County. The casino has two restaurants, the Creekside Café and Legends Fine Dining. The entire casino enterprise provides revenues to support tribal programs and other economic development projects.

The people of the southern Puget Sound waterways carved petroglyphs depicting fish or other animals, mountains, and a series of circles. The petroglyph known as the Love Rock was taken from Harstine Island in the 1970s and is now displayed at Tumwater Falls Park near Olympia. Its name stems from a legend that hundreds of years ago Squaxin Island couples sat on the rock looking out over the moonlit waters. Another petroglyph removed from Eld Inlet is currently at the Washington State Capital Museum. This petroglyph depicts a face, and there are several interpretations as to whether it is that of a human or another type of animal. Although these two petroglyphs have been removed, others remain in their original, protected locations.

SUGGESTED READING

The Squaxin Island Tribe is the sole authority of its cultural knowledge, which outside writers have attempted to interpret. The following works provide additional information but may contain misinterpretations.

Castile, George P., ed. 1985. *The Indians of Puget Sound: The Notebooks of Myron Eells.* Seattle: University of Washington Press; Walla Walla, Wash.: Whitman College.
Meeker, Ezra. 1905. *The Tragedy of Leschi.* Reprint. Seattle: Museum of History and Industry, 1980.
Morgan, Murray. 1981. *Puget's Sound: A Narrative of Early Tacoma and the Southern Sound.* Seattle: University of Washington Press.

James Barr, Beatrice Black, and Joe DeLaCruz playing *pala*. *Pala* means "sprouting up" and is a game that was played around the longhouse. A fern is picked and each person takes turns saying "pala," as they go up and down the fern, touching each leaf without hesitation. Quinault Archives.

Quinault

Justine E. James, Jr.
with Leilani A. Chubby

The creation of the Quinault people and the occupation of their land date back to the birth of the ocean, land, and sky. Quinault legend describes the creation of the world in three distinct phases. In the beginning, Wha-neh wha-neh, the great giver of life, created the forces of nature—clouds, mountains, ocean, rivers, and sky—as people. The second phase is the time when animals and birds possessed the same characteristics as people and they coexisted as equals. Finally, during the third phase, Misp' the Transformer, traveled throughout the land and changed the animals, birds, land features, and people into their present form and way of life (Patterson 1968: 27–30). Before the arrival of humans, only supernatural creatures, the magical animals, inhabited the earth. The Great Spirit called the magical animals together in a great council and disclosed that he wanted to place human creatures on the earth. He described them and said he would name them "Quinault," which means "the People" (Meyers 1994: 86).

Cultural History

Today the Quinault tribal membership includes seven distinct groups—Quinault, Quileute, Queets, Hoh, Chehalis, Chinook, Cowlitz—and many subbands that have been absorbed or lost individual identity. Of these, only the Quinault and Queets were original inhabitants of the present-day Quinault territory, which encompasses the Quinault and Queets watersheds and the coastline. The Quinault people also had settlements beyond this area, at Chenois Creek, Oyhut, and Copalis, to name a few. However, much of the traditional Quinault territory was negotiated away by the government through the Quinault River Treaty of 1855.

The name Quinault stems from k^{w}ínayɬ, the Quinault word for the largest village at the mouth of the Quinault River. This was a familial village, located and named for its inhabitants by the British fur trader Capt. Charles William Barkley in 1787. Quinault has since become the recognized spelling for the members of the Quinault Indian Nation and the reservation. The village of Quinault is now called Taholah, named after the Quinault chief Taxola, who was one of the signatories to the treaty of 1855. Taholah is also the seat of the present-day tribal government.

The northern Quinault Reservation village of Queets is named for a distinct group that inhabited the area of the Queets River system. Similar to the origin of the name Quinault, Queets is derived from q^{w}ícx^w. The following is the creation story of the Queets Tribe:

> The Great Spirit waded across the river. Upon reaching the other side he stopped to rub his legs to restore circulation. He then threw the rolls of dirt, which came from his legs and they landed in the River. Out came a man and a woman to form the Qu-itz-qu tribe. The tribal name translates to "out of the dirt of the skin." (Hodge 1907–10: 2:101)

Although the Queets people are a distinct social group, they spoke the same Coast Salish language as the Quinault but with a slightly different dialect (Thompson and Kinkade 1990: 38). All tribal groups in the Quinault Indian Nation are referred to in this chapter as Quinault.

The daily life of the Quinault revolved around the abundant food found in the area. The kexnaxx'el (people) traveled to the mountains, prairies, and seashores in search of berries, fish, game, and medicinal plants. An intricate trail system throughout the Olympic Peninsula greatly facilitated these pursuits and frequent social interaction with other tribes. The trails were an important economic route for trading and exchange with tribes across the Olympic Mountains and into the area of Puget Sound (Olson 1936: 17; Storm et al. 1990: 68).

In spite of their frequent travels to gather nature's bounty, the Quinault had permanent village sites along the riverbanks where they harvested and processed seasonal runs of salmon. Before the treaty, there were approximately fifty-five known village sites, the majority located along the banks of the Quinault and Queets Rivers. A number of seasonal residential sites were also located around Lake Quinault, particularly at the confluence of large creeks on the south side of the lake. Others extended to the upper reaches of the Quinault and Queets Rivers. The Lake Quinault sites were selected because of the relatively low flat deltas that provided access to the sockeye runs.

Queets design. Quinault Archives.

The Quinault traveled primarily along the waterways because of the dense forests and vegetation. Like other tribes of the Northwest Coast, they developed a unique water transportation system using the dugout canoe. These canoes were carved from a single old-growth cedar tree harvested from the temperate rain forest. There were a variety of dugout canoes, depending on the waterway and the function. For example, a double bow dugout canoe, often referred to as the shovel nose canoe, was used on rivers because of its ability to maneuver the currents and slide over logjams. Ocean transportation and whale hunting required a much larger canoe that could cut through ocean waves and carry larger loads. The photo-historian Ralph Andrews (1956: 76) noted that "the Quinault constructed very superior canoes, with high bows and sterns, many of them could carry fifty to sixty people. In addition they sold and traded the canoes with tribes in the Puget Sound and Columbia River regions."

The Quinault excelled at canoe travel, as the Seattle Press Expedition recognized at the end of their six-month journey over the Olympics. In May 1890, after crossing the Olympic Mountains, the expedition reached the Quinault River and tried to float down in a handcrafted raft. The raft floated into a fallen tree and capsized. The men felt very lucky to survive and to retrieve their field notes and maps. Soon after this incident, a Quinault canoe was returning downriver from the fork of the south and main stem. The Quinault picked up the expedition members and brought them all the way to Taholah. Charles Barnes wrote of the Quinault's abilities:

> In the hands of the Indians, who had been brought up from boyhood on the river, and had frequently traveled as high as the forks, the voyage was made in perfect safety. Their knowledge of the current is wonderful. They know every submerged sandbar, rock, and snag on the river, and just the right stroke of the paddle at the right time sends the canoe past dangers which to us were invisible until we were by them. (Cited in Wood 1989: 194)

One of the Quinault canoeists who brought the Press Expedition safely downriver was Frederick Pope, the son of the famous shaman Bob Pope. In 1913 and 1920 Bob Pope, who was quite elderly by this time, transported Mountaineer expeditions down the river (Meany 1920: 34).

Today modes of water transportation have changed primarily to skiffs, larger ocean vessels, and modified canoes with outboard motors. However, the traditional dugout canoes are still carved and used in cultural celebrations and ocean journeys.

Canoes not only served as a mode of transportation; they were also used in the sport of racing. Whether paddled or motorized, canoe racing has been an integral part of Quinault history since the early 1900s. The shovel nose canoe was used in a special logjam canoe race. The objective was to get the canoe over the logjam while the men stayed inside the canoe. Starting from the stern, the men stood and moved quickly toward the middle of the canoe. When they got the canoe halfway over the log, they ran quickly to the bow to weigh it down, and then the canoe rolled over the log and the men paddled to the finish line (Bennett interview). Another type of race, involving the eleven-man war canoe, was conducted until 1934 and began on Lake Quinault. Today the practice of canoe racing continues with such events as the skiff race, the powder-puff race, the two-person capsize, and paddling. Flat-bottom canoes outfitted with modified outboard motors are also used in races. Many races are held during the Chief Taholah Days celebration on the July Fourth weekend.

An important aspect of Quinault culture was the longhouse. These multifamily homes served as more than mere protection from the elements; they were also education centers for youth:

> Every morning before grandmother would tell the children stories and teach them, old grandfather would go to the east side of the long house and open one of the boards and the sun would come in. He'd pray to the man behind the daylight that everything they did that day would be right and that the man behind the daylight would take care of them. (Sotomish interview)

Traditional Quinault longhouses were large, rectangular dwellings constructed of adzed planks from the *ch'item*, or western red cedar, with common Northwest-style gable roofs (Olson 1936: 29, 31; Storm et al. 1990: 53).

Many families resided in a single household, which provided many teachers. As children grew up, they learned about all aspects of Quinault life, including weaving, tool construction, carving, hunting, fishing, and other skills. Elders were the main instructors of language, oral history, legends, plant use, and social development. This type of extended family education provided young people with survival skills and intellectual challenges; it also encouraged cooperation and community support through the study of the natural environment and legends:

> Every morning our uncle would take us down to the river and have us jump into the water seven times to cleanse our body. Each time we returned from the water our uncle would be sitting by the fire. If we tried to stand by the fire he would tell us, "Oh, you don't baby yourself, you have to make your body strong," and he'd make us stay away from the fire. (Sotomish interview)

The most important cultural resource and economic staple of the Quinault people is the salmon, especially the sockeye known as the blueback. A Quinault legend told by Bob Pope explains the origin of the blueback and how the Quinault came to enjoy this precious gift:

> While journeying in the ocean they came upon the smoke of a large village [beyond the western horizon], and as they neared it saw that the smoke was of different colors, and that from the middle of the village rose a great column of reddish smoke, and they steered for this. . . . And the place turned out to be the home of the salmon. All kinds of salmon lived there, and each kind of salmon had a different smoke. And the reddish smoke belonged to the bluebacks. (Cited in Farrand 1902: 112)

The cultural importance of the salmon is represented in a number of traditional customs, including the first salmon ceremony. The salmon must be treated with honor and respect so that they will return to the place of their birth. The Quinault understand that they are not simply the beneficiaries of the salmon as food; they also have responsibilities to carry out the practices of their ancestors.

Salmon are anadromous; that is, they live in both freshwater and salt water. The young salmon migrate to the ocean for three to five years, feeding and maturing before an internal biological clock summons them to return to the river of their birth. The salmon begin their river ascent when conditions, such as rain, water temperature, and water depth, are favorable. On reaching their destination, the female deposits her eggs into a gravel nest, called a redd, that she has prepared with her tail. Then a male, swimming at her side, fertilizes the eggs. Just as the act of spawning assures life for new generations, it also completes the life cycle for most adult salmon species.

The steelhead, once considered a trout by the scientific community, is now classified as a Pacific salmon. Steelhead are the only salmon that survive to return to the ocean after spawning (Storm et al. 1990: 56). The Quinault used steelhead eggs to make a delicacy known as "stink eggs." In 1889 Indian agent Charles Willoughby (1889: 269) documented a method for preparing the delicious cheeselike dish. The eggs are placed into a box or barrel and allowed to ferment: in time they are ready to eat. As a result of a fatal salmonella outbreak in 1964, as well as dietary changes, stink eggs are no longer consumed.

Of the six salmon species found in the Quinault and Queets watersheds—the chinook (king), chum (dog), coho (silver), pink (humpback), sockeye (blueback), and steelhead—the sockeye (Quinault blueback) is most significant. The Quinault and Ozette are the only two rivers on the Olympic Peninsula that provide the essential habitat for sockeye salmon. The two watersheds contain lakes where the sockeye fry live during their early years, before smolting for their ocean journey. The flavor, texture, and superior qualities of the Quinault River blueback are so highly regarded that they have been a major item of Quinault culture, trade, and commerce for centuries.

In the past salmon were harvested by a number of techniques that varied according to location. After entering the river, the salmon stop feeding and live off their stored fat until they spawn and then die. Therefore, hooks were not practical; instead, dragnets, weirs, spears, gill nets, gaffs, traps, and dip nets were used. The fishnets were fabricated from the stinging nettle plant, which grows prolifically in this region and made strong cordage. The stalks were cut, split, dried, and beaten so the fiber could be teased apart, and then spun into twine by rolling it between the palm and thigh.

The dragnet or drift net was weighted and secured to four long poles held by four fishers in two canoes. The net was pulled along the river until fish could be felt within it, and then it was quickly hauled into the canoe. Today's fishers no longer use either the dragnet or drift net technique for fishing (Olson 1936: 85–86).

Weirs were essentially fences through which water flowed. The support pilings for some of these structures were permanent and held latticework that could be used in two ways: by diverting migrating salmon into some type of trap or by concentrating the fish into a narrow, shallow area where they could be speared or dip netted. Once the fishers obtained enough salmon for winter stores, the weirs were opened to allow the salmon to continue their upstream spawning migration.

Today fishers are assigned specific fishing grounds. At these locations, they place semipermanent hemlock stakes into the river bottom and affix gill nets made of synthetic nylon. This is a more durable and lightweight product than the former nettle nets. The fishing grounds are located throughout the lower river up to the five-mile tidal influence boundary. Many of the fishing grounds are hereditary, but the river committee assigns others. The fishers usually work their assigned sites, but they are at liberty to employ another fisher to manage their ground for a percentage of the catch. Maintenance of a fishing ground may require removal of debris such as stumps, trees, and root wads.

The Quinault also relied on the ocean and seashore for food. The razor clam was harvested at Point Grenville, Roosevelt, Kalaloch, and Copalis beaches; other mollusks were collected from the rocky promontories at Point Grenville and Cape Elizabeth; and crab was taken all along the coastline. Mollusks continue to be a very important food product for the Quinault people today.

Ducks, geese, gulls, and loons were regularly hunted for food, and gull eggs were collected in the summer to provide nourishment and variety in the diet. Tribal elder Nina Bumgarner commented that "there are too many seagulls today because we do not collect and eat the eggs as we did in the olden days" (Cited in Storm et al. 1990: 123).

The Quinault were the southernmost whaling tribe on the Northwest Coast. Successful hunts depended greatly on religious and cultural influences, including spiritual assistance. Spirit powers were obtained through dreams, visions, and spirit quests. Any number of guardian spirits could bless a hunter, and each endowed its host with special skills, but only a few Quinault sea hunters possessed the special spirit power necessary to hunt whales (Olson 1936: 12, 143–51). In 1937 Washington Howeattle of Queets stated that he had not hunted a whale in more than thirty years. In a newspaper article he related the following:

In the canoe whaling days Whale Creek, within a few rods of the mouth of Raft River, supplied a particularly advantageous inlet. It cut a deep channel well out to sea, and by the right sort of manipulation a good whaler could steer his victim into this channel, decoy it toward shore. Thus the victim often gave his killers a free ride home and obligingly piled himself up on the beach, where at low tide he could be properly attended to. (*Yakima Herald* 1937)

The Quinault also hunted seals, sea otters, and sea lions. The last recorded sea lion hunt was in 1905. The sea mammal hunter required not only special powers and skill but also patience and the ability to remain absolutely quiet:

> The old-style seal skin seats would creak when they dried. So that's when they switched over to cedar seats with pegs. . . . [Otherwise] the seals would hear the canoe coming because of the creaking noise. (Williams 1995: 6)

Some Quinault practiced small-scale agriculture after the reservation was established. Historically, they used controlled burns to modify the environment. Prairies were burned to ensure that camas and other favorite species such as berries and ferns would grow. The Quinault possessed a unique relationship and understanding of the plants within their territory and used them for medicine and tools as well as food (Storm et al. 1990: 62–65).

Clam digging. Quinault Archives.

Nina Bumgardner. Photo by Josef Scaylea.

EUROPEAN CONTACT

According to written records, the Quinault were the first Native Americans of present-day Washington State to have made contact with Europeans. On July 14, 1775, the frigate *Santiago*, with the Spanish naval officer Bruno de Hezeta, and the schooner *Sonora*, commanded by Juan de Ayala and Juan Francisco Bodega y Quadra, were anchored along the coast of Quinault territory. Early in the "morning a canoe with nine Indians approached the Frigate [*Santiago*], making gestures of friendship, and inviting [the crew] to go to their settlement. . . . They gave [the sailors] some fish and exchanged some otter skins." (Wagner and Baker 1930: 227).

At about the same time the captain of the *Santiago*, the Franciscan chaplain, Fray Benito de la Sierra, the pilot, the surgeon, and twenty armed men went ashore at Point Grenville to "take possession of the land" for Spain, which was done in "haste and without mass being said" because of the weather and concerns for the *Santiago*'s position (Wagner and Baker 1930: 227). Even without mass, the ceremony included the planting of a cross and a bottle and the etching of a cross into a rock (Storm et al. 1990: 86).

A league to the north of the *Santiago*, the crew of the *Sonora* had anchored near shore. The day before the Indians had traded fish and whale meat with the sailors, for which the Indians received "some trifles." The next morning the Indians again visited, and "the chief [brought] his wife and two other women, who were given presents" (Wagner and Baker 1930: 227). Soon after, a party of seven men from the *Sonora* went ashore to get water and cut a topmast, and five of the men were attacked and killed by "Indians who had been watching" from the forest (ibid.: 228). The two other crewmen fled, and most probably drowned. The Indians then took iron and other pieces from the boat. The remaining men on the *Sonora* killed six or seven Indians in retribution for the lives of the seven Spaniards. The two Spanish crews decided to set sail while they had a wind, and they left the area at three o'clock that afternoon (ibid.: 229; Storm et al. 1990: 87).

To this day experts continue to speculate about the exact location[1] and motive for this attack, as there had been only friendly interaction and trading before the incident. However, claiming the land for Spain surely did not go unnoticed by the people who already held "possession" of the land. The ceremony marking this event was led by a chaplain who placed a cross in the ground and began to pray. The significance of such a "medicine man" in a black robe would have been construed as a significant event of religious power on Quinault land, or perhaps the Quinault thought that the Black Klokwalle spirits from the ocean had come to torment them (Storm et al. 1990: 84, 86).

Although there are discrepancies regarding the exact location of the *Sonora*'s fateful encounter, it is possible that one of the ships entered a women's safe haven, which could explain the surprising change to hostile behavior and the resulting deaths. More likely, we will never know what precipitated the events of that day.

The number of European contacts with the Quinault gradually increased to include occasional visits by English and Russian traders and explorers, until the signing of the treaty in 1855 and subsequent settlement of the area.

POLITICAL HISTORY

The most significant political event in Quinault history came with the signing of the treaty. In July 1855 representatives for territorial governor Stevens met at the mouth of the Quinault River with the Hoh, Queets, Quileute, and Quinault tribal leaders to negotiate the Quinault River Treaty, which became known as the Treaty of Olympia when Stevens signed it several months later, on January 25, 1856, in Olympia. This treaty ceded to the United States nearly one-third of the Olympic Peninsula, an estimated 1.2 million acres, in exchange for a "tract or tracts of land sufficient for their wants" and guarantees such as the "right of taking fish at all usual and accustomed grounds and stations" (12 Stat. 971; July 1, 1855, and January 25, 1856) (Storm et al. 1990: 282).

The Quinault Reservation was subsequently expanded by executive order on November 4, 1873. Despite treaty guarantees, subsequent acts of Congress resulted in the loss of Quinault Reservation land. The most devastating was the Dawes, or General Allotment, Act of 1887. The purpose of the Dawes Act was to divide tribally owned communal lands into individual allotments for farming and grazing purposes. After a twenty-five-year period, the land would be taken out of trust status and the allottee would acquire title and become a U.S. citizen.

The allotment process ended when all potential agricultural land along the river was allotted in 1912. In 1924 a federal district court ruled that those who had not yet received allotments should have the right to land, even if it was more valuable for timber than agriculture, and 1,650 new allotments were issued (Ullman, Lane, and Smith 1977: 64).

A congressional act in 1911 declared that the Hoh, Quileute, Ozette, and other tribes affiliated with the Quinault and Quileute in the treaty had the right to allotments on the Quinault Reservation. This act did not include the tribes to the south of the Quinault who were party to a failed March 1855 treaty negotiation at the mouth of the Chehalis River. These tribes believed they too should have allotments on the Quinault Reservation and took their case to the U. S. Supreme Court in 1932. The Court ruled that the Chehalis, Chinook, Cowlitz, and other tribes who never located on reservations were also eligible for allotments under the 1911 act. The last of the 2,340 individual allotments were issued and approved by 1933, leaving no tribally owned or surplus land on the reservation (Reis 1987: 67; Storm et al. 1990: 173–7). Today the Quinault Reservation includes not only tribal members but also nonmembers with allotments, many of whom live elsewhere (Ullman, Lane, and Smith 1977: 69).

The adverse effects of the allotment policy included allotment of reservation lands to non-Quinault tribal members, nonresident allottees, sale of tribal lands after the trust period to timber companies, and the "sale by the government of heirship lands (with multiple owners) to settle estates" (Ullman, Lane, and Smith 1977: 18). In 1906 Congress passed the Burke Act, which allowed the secretary of the interior to end the trust status of individual allottees. At any time the secretary of the interior could issue a fee simple patent or title to tribal allotments, if the tribal member was judged "competent" to manage his or her own affairs. The intent of this act was to offer quick access to land patents, in the hope of alleviating the problem of fractionalization of allotments that occurred when allottees died intestate, whereupon their trust parcels were divided and subdivided among numerous heirs (Deloria 1983: 28–29).

Commissioner of Indian Affairs John Collier drew on a 1928 government report, *The Problem of Indian Administration* (1928) by Lewis Meriam, and some of his own ideas for cultural renewal to write the Indian Reorganization Act of 1934. The IRA ended the allotment of tribal lands and extended the trust period indefinitely if the landowner did not request a fee patent. It also enabled the tribe to organize for the common welfare of its members and adopt federally approved constitutions and bylaws. The goal of the IRA was to focus power on the reservation, not in Washington, D.C. (Bestor 1971: 67; Deloria 1983 :12–15; Storm et al. 1990: 190).

THE QUINAULT INDIAN NATION TODAY

The Quinault Indian Nation is one of a handful of tribes in the United States that chose not to organize under the Indian Reorganization Act of 1934. The tribe created and adopted the *Bylaws of the General Council of the Indians of the Quinault Indian Reservation* in 1922 (amended in 1974). Then, in 1975, the general tribal membership approved a constitution to form the foundation of the current Quinault Indian Nation government.

The Quinault Indian Nation's governing body consists of a business committee of eleven elected council members, including president, vice president, secretary, treasurer, and seven council members. The business committee is elected annually, and each member serves a staggered three-year term (Storm et al. 1990: 209–10; Wells 1997: 8).

In 1990 the Quinault Nation was one of seven tribes to negotiate a tribal compact under the Self-Governance Demonstration Project. Self-governance allows the tribe to plan, conduct, and administer its own programs and deal directly with the federal government rather than the Bureau of Indian Affairs. The major advantage of tribal self-governance is that the Quinault are allowed to make funding decisions and allocations to tribal programs based on local needs. The Self-Governance Demonstration Project became permanent law in 1994. It has contributed to a stronger relationship between the tribe and county, state, and federal agencies and has allowed the tribe to employ more Quinault tribal members in administrative positions. In a speech on self-determination, President Clinton spoke of the federal government's relationship to tribes:

> Long ago, many of your ancestors gave up land, water, and mineral rights in exchange for peace, security, health care, [and] education from the federal government. It is a solemn pact. And while the United States government did not live up to its side of the bargain in the past, we can and must honor it today and into that new millennium. (Clinton 1998)

Reservation Community

There are three communities on the reservation, Taholah, Queets, and Amanda Park. Taholah has the largest population, followed by Queets. Amanda Park, at the southwestern end of Lake Quinault, has a predominantly non-Indian population of about 190 (Wells 1997: 9).

In 1997 there were 479 residences on the reservation, up from 89 in 1943. This additional housing has allowed many tribal members to return to their homeland (Patterson 1967: 10). Since 1955 the on-reservation population has increased from 400 to approximately 1,500, with tribal enrollment approaching 2,900.

A BIA boarding school was constructed at Taholah in the early 1860s. The federal government permitted a variety of religious sects to assume command of the agency, the school, and medical facility. The BIA believed that the "civilization" of the Indians, or separating them from their Indian ways, would be hastened through instruction in Western religion and the English language and a livelihood based on agriculture. The local boarding school

President Clinton greeting Kalvin Valdillez, a member of the Quinault Tribe at Tillicum Village, Seattle, during the 1993 Asia Pacific Economic Cooperation meeting. Quinault Archives.

operated into the mid-1950s and was replaced in 1956 by Taholah Public School District 77, kindergarten through sixth grade. A few families opted to have their children attend Indian boarding schools in Oregon, California, and Oklahoma.

The Taholah and Queets-Clearwater public schools provided education only for the elementary grades, and the middle and high school students traveled to the Moclips or Lake Quinault school districts. In 1972 the Taholah Education Center expanded the reservation school system to include middle school, and a high school was added in 1991. The Taholah High School football team, the Chitwhins (the Quinault word for "Bear") won the state B-8 division championship in 1997.

Current Issues

A crucial program for the Quinault Indian Nation is reacquiring land inside the external boundaries of the reservation. This program is outlined in the tribe's comprehensive plan and has increased tribal landownership on the reservation from 7 to 30 percent since 1988 (Wells 1997: 14). The goals of the land management division on the Quinault Reservation are fivefold: (1) reduce the amount of fee patent ownership; (2) increase the tribal trust land base; (3) arrest fractionation of trust properties; (4) assist with the management of tribal landownership, easements, rights-of way, leases, and nontimber resources; and (5) provide baseline information to trust landowners.

The Quinault Department of Natural Resources (QDNR) is a major employer on the reservation and consists of three divisions: Forestry, Environmental Protection, and Fisheries. QDNR ensures the conservation, enhancement, preservation, and productivity of all resources within reservation boundaries and traditionally used resources off-reservation.

The forestry division protects and manages Quinault forestlands, which have suffered from years of poor harvesting practices. The forestry division is working to regenerate and restore the forest while managing for sustainable timber harvest and specialized forest products.

The mission of the environmental protection division is to maintain the integrity of the Quinault Indian Nation for the continued prosperity of its members. The division works with private, state, and federal agencies and timber companies to protect the habitat that sustains salmon and wildlife and to ensure compliance with environmental laws.

To perpetuate the tribes' fishing heritage, the Quinault fisheries division continues to provide harvest management, hatchery production, and technical services. Harvest management, a vital component of the fisheries program, provides current biological information and technical guidance to manage and regulate the fisheries. In addition, there is an enhancement program, which is responsible for artificial enhancement and habitat restoration. The Quinault fisheries operate and maintain fishery enhancement facilities on the Quinault Reservation. The Lake Quinault Hatchery (pen rearing) provides fish for the Quinault River and other coastal streams. The Salmon River fish culture facility provides fish for the Queets River system. Enhancement personnel also provide technical support to the U.S. Fish and Wildlife Service's Quinault National Fish Hatchery at Cook Creek. Tribal members employed by the Fish and Wildlife Service staff this facility. The tribal fisheries program also has a stock assessment program, responsible for assessment and monitoring of salmon and shellfish. The staff collects important data vital to salmon and shellfish management, including population estimates for razor clams, halibut, black cod, and Dungeness crab and toxin monitoring of shellfish and crab.

In the late 1960s and early 1970s the tribe began steelhead and salmon monitoring to track the number of fish returning to the Quinault River. This effort led to the development of the Quinault Pride seafood processing plant that supplies a worldwide market of salmon and seafood products. Quinault Pride finances loans to tribal fishers for ocean vessels involved in the crab and sea-fishing industry. In 1997 the Quinault Indian Nation acquired the marina at Ocean Shores to moor the growing tribal fleet of oceangoing fishing vessels.

The Quinault Nation encourages tribal members to pursue educational opportunities. The nation has developed outreach educational programs with Northwest Indian College, Grays Harbor College, and Evergreen State College[2] that offer tribal members the opportunity to acquire a technical or liberal arts degree in satellite classes and college courses while maintaining jobs on the reservation.

Heritage Programs

The Quinault Nation's cultural coordinator works to ensure the perpetuation and appreciation of tribal culture through maintenance of the archive, library, and museum and through classes, presentations, and documentation of Quinault history and culture.

The Taholah Education Center offers cultural enrichment classes such as Quinault language, history, and traditional skills. Realizing that children are the future of the tribe, Head Start has implemented a program to ensure that they are introduced to the language and traditions of the Quinault. The tribal goal is to provide more direction for their most important resource, the children, and to improve Indian education.

Tribal members have formed dance and song groups that participate in a variety of activities, including blessings, dancing, and singing at community events and marriage, funeral, memorial, and name-giving ceremonies.

The Quinault's traditional homeland continues to be a focus of Quinault culture. Fishing on the ocean, beaches, and rivers is a cultural activity that reinforces personal and tribal identity and also provides nourishment. Each year the Quinault people travel to various sites on and off the reservation to gather basketry materials, cedar bark, bear grass, cattail, sweetgrass, and beach grass, as the Quinault people have done for hundreds of years. Plants and roots are gathered during specific seasons and used as remedies for colds, aches attributed to arthritis, and other afflictions. The Quinault people are acutely aware of these special gifts and thank the Creator for his offerings.

The following poem composed in the 1960s by Quinault cultural representative Clarence Pickernell describes the tribes' association to their homeland:

THIS IS MY LAND
This is my land.
From the time of the first moon, till the time of the last sun.
It was given to my people.
Wha-neh wha-neh, the great giver of life, made me out of the earth of this land.
He said, "You are the land, and the land is you."
I take well care of this land, for I am part of it.
I take well care of the animals, for they are my brothers and sisters.
I take care of the streams and rivers, for they clean the land.
I honor Ocean as my father, for he gives me food and a means of travel.
Ocean knows everything, for he is everywhere.
Ocean is wise, for he is old.
Listen to Ocean, for he speaks wisdom. He sees much, and knows more. He
    says, "Take care of my sister, Earth.
She is young and has little wisdom, but much kindness.
When she smiles, it is springtime.
Scar not her beauty, for she is beautiful beyond all things.
Her face looks eternally upward to the sky and stars, where she once lived with
    her father, Sky."
I am forever grateful for this beautiful and bountiful earth.
God gave it to me.
This is my land.

The relationship with the land, the animals, and the ocean expressed in this poem demonstrates legends have contemporary relevance. The concept of a personified Ocean who talks with animals is not an anomaly. Spirits continue to have human attributes, and spirits are all around us.

Visitor Opportunities

The largest event of the year is held during the July Fourth holiday. The Chief Taholah Days celebration commemorates the July 1, 1855, signing of the treaty with the Quinault. The celebration is open to the public, and activities include the crowning of Miss Quinault Indian Nation, a parade, outboard canoe races, a traditional salmon bake, water and field sports, softball tournaments, and a fireworks display.

Although the Quinault Reservation has certain restrictions regarding access by nontribal members, the tribe offers a number of activities for visitors:

- Guided fishing trips for perch, steelhead, and trout on the lower Quinault River.
- Trout fishing on Lake Quinault, authorized with a tribal license available at Amanda Park Mercantile and Rain Forest Resort at Lake Quinault. (Subject to tribal conservation closures.)
- Beach hiking with a day pass from the tribal police department or the tribal administration office.
- The Quinault Pride seafood plant offers freshly caught salmon, smoked salmon packages, or seafood gift packs. The seafood store is located at 100 Quinault Street, Taholah.
- The mercantile stores offer fuel, deli foods, snacks, and tribal arts and crafts.
- The Quinault Indian Nation Recreation Program sponsors the Point Grenville surfing contest the last weekend of August.
- Visitors may tour the Quinault National Fish Hatchery at Cook Creek. The facility includes a visitor center and is usually open seven days a week from 8:00 A.M. to 4:30 P.M.
- Visitors are welcome at the tribal museum to view the exhibits, crafts, carvings, and historical publications. The museum is open from 9:00 A.M. to 4:30 P.M. weekdays. Tours should be scheduled in advance.
- The marina at Ocean Shores, L'akmaltch (Owns Harbor), has a boat launch and moorage, a convenience store, an RV park with hookups, and a passenger-only ferry service across the harbor to Westport. E-mail marina@techline.com.
- The Quinault Beach Resort and Casino is located directly on the beach near Ocean Shores. The facility has 150 guest rooms, a full-service spa, a fitness room, and a swimming pool, as well as an activity room for education and recreation. The resort has a state-of-the-art facility for meetings, banquets, and special events. Emily's restaurant features Northwest cuisine and an adjoining cabaret with live musical entertainment. In addition, the international-style casino features electronic gaming machines and a complete array of table games. The Internet web site for the resort is Quinaultbchresort.com.

NOTES

1. See Storm et al. 1980: 83–88 for a summary of the possible locations.
2. The Quinault Indian Nation wishes to commend Carol Minugh for conceptualizing this unique educational opportunity.

SUGGESTED READING

Jones, Joan Megan. 1977. *Basketry of the Quinault.* Taholah, Wash.: Quinault Indian
    Nation.
Olson, Ronald. 1936. *The Quinault Indians.* Seattle: University of Washington Press.
Storm, Jacqueline M., David Chance, Jim Harp, Karen Harp, Lawrence Lesteele,
    Sarah Colleen Sotomish, and Larry Workman. 1990. *The Land of the Quinault.*
    Taholah, Wash.: Quinault Indian Nation.

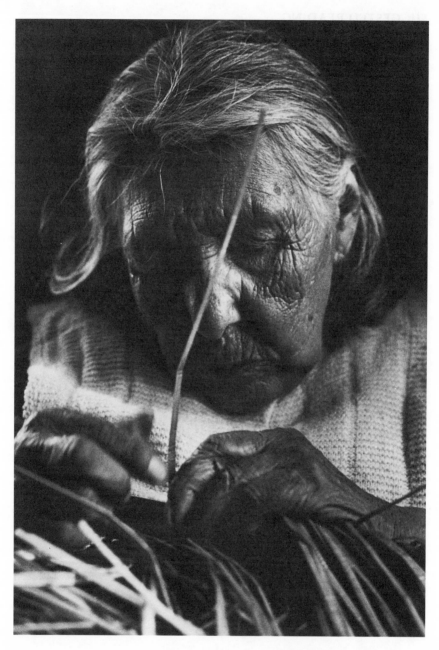
Mattie Howeattle. Photo by Josef Scaylea.

Hoh

Viola Riebe and Helen Lee

The Hoh were created at the Time of Beginnings by K'wati, the shape-shifting Changer who went around the world making things as they are today. When K'wati got to the Hoh River, he discovered that the inhabitants were upside-down people who walked on their hands and handled their fishnets clumsily with their feet. They were not very good at it, so they were hungry and skinny. K'wati set them right side up and showed them how to operate their nets with their hands. In the Hoh language, the word *p'ip'isodac'iłi* means "upside-down people." According to the linguist Manuel Andrade (1931: 85), as recorded in *Quileute Texts*, after Changer set them upright, he told the people, "You shall use your feet to walk. . . . Go and fish smelt. You shall catch much fish when you fish smelt." Ever since then there has been a lot of smelt at the Hoh.

Cultural History

The Hoh people call themselves *chalat'*, "the ones who live on the Hoh." The river gets its name from the Quinault word *hoxʷ*, but the Hoh word for the river is *chalak'ac'it*. Their artful navigation of the fifty-mile river allowed them to reach village and fishing sites, hunting encampments, and places where they could harvest plants and other resources. The beaches to the north and south of the river mouth and the ocean promontories and islands also supplied the Hoh with sustenance.

The old people believed that every person had both a soul and a spirit power (*t'axilit*). All living things had souls, so ceremonies were held to thank the soul of the salmon and the steelhead; the elk, deer, and bear; the whale,

by Rachel Dreher Hoh tribe 1998 4th g.

Drawing of Upside-down Person by Rachel Dreher, 1998.

seal, and sea lion; and the great cedars, which they used for canoes, house planks, and much more. Rituals were carried out to perpetuate the salmon, for example. All of the bones of the first salmon caught by each family were put back in the water with grateful thanks. This first salmon ritual is still conducted by many families.

If the salmon or other animals were offended, they might withhold themselves from the fishers and hunters, which could affect the entire village. There might be famine if the salmon did not run upriver or the elk went elsewhere or hid from hunters. Therefore, the whole tribe was on the lookout for behavior that was known to be offensive or spiritually unpredictable. There were literally hundreds of taboos that were relevant to the traditional worldview.

A person's *t'axilit* could be inherited at birth from an ancestor or by reincarnation. It provided the person with talent and helped him or her to learn new skills and accomplish great things. One might acquire additional spirit powers by going out questing. For example, gambling spirits, whaling and sealing spirits, doctoring spirits, and weathermen's spirits could all be sought. Seal hunters imitated the seal by rolling around on sharp rocks along the coast, which brought them closer to the seal spirit. Whale hunters went into caves and swam like whales to seek their help (Daugherty 1948–49). Those who had specific spirit powers could join secret spirit dance societies: the oily voiced society (for whalers), the elk dance society (for hunters), the fish club society (for fishermen), the southern song society (for warriors), the second-sight society (people who had the power to predict the weather or "find" the body of someone who had drowned), and the doctoring society.

The relation of spirit powers to subsistence in the traditional perspective is very clear. In Hoh traditional belief, the supreme spirit was T'sik'ati, Nature Spirit. Morning prayers of thanks and hope are directed to T'sik'ati and sometimes to the "grandfathers," the ghosts of ancestors.

A canoe maker would observe various taboos and ceremonies of gratitude to the great tree that he was going to hew, lest the tree be offended and not allow itself to be made into a canoe that would go straight or stay afloat. Although many types of wood were used, the cedar was revered because it was easy to split. It was used for houses, canoes, large carved house posts, and welcoming figures. Cedar bark was an important weaving material, but various other grasses, reeds, and roots, which were dried, split, dyed, and woven, were also used by the exceptional basket weavers.

In the old days on the Hoh, foods were preserved and stored for the inclement winter months. Pansy Howeattle Hudson once said, "We used to eat everything edible from the mountains to the ocean depths. Sometimes in the afternoon, dinner was whatever was on the beach" (quoted in Powell 1969). The people of the Hoh were attuned to the cycle of life's bounty, as noted by the anthropologist Richard Daugherty (1948-49: 3:85), "When the flowers bloom on the elderberries they know the first run of spring kings will begin—this is the signal to set the trap."

All settlement sites had a fish trap, or weir, that had an opening through which migrating fish passed as the fisherman waited with his net or spear. When the families lower on the river had the fish they needed, the weir would be opened so that people farther upriver could fill their needs.

The Hoh River was one of the best places along the coast to catch smelt. The surf in early summer was alive with silver and night smelt, and as many as one hundred pounds could be taken in a single dip (Daugherty 1948–49: 2:26). Along the beach, clams, barnacles, mussels, sea urchins, crabs, anemones, China slippers, and sea cucumbers were collected. The eggs of seagulls and other birds, such as the sea parrot (puffin), were gathered on the rock promontories. The eggs were eaten fresh or hard-boiled (Daugherty 1948–49: 1:111).

Set net fishing on the Hoh. Photo by Ruth Kirk.

The Hoh hunted elk, deer, bear, cougar, bobcat, and smaller game. One method of elk hunting mentioned by Herbert Fisher is intriguing.

> They say that they used to put cedar bark on a runway that they have on the mountains over there, lay it on the trail, you know, that is steep just like that. Put the bark there upside down, and once they step on that they slide down and they always follow the leader, you know, elk. Another one comes along and down it goes, way down. That is how they get them, no gun. (Powell field notes 1988)

Traditional hunters used a wide variety of equipment and techniques: bow and arrow, lances, clubs, deadfalls, pitfalls, and spring and loop snares.

The Hoh were also proficient sea mammal hunters. In canoes of various sizes, people hunted whales, sea lions, and fur and hair seals. As many as twenty or thirty sealing canoes would head to sea at one time. The seal hunter stayed up all night to watch the weather. The sealing canoe left before daybreak with a captain, a spearman, and a third crewman. They watched the surf closely. If it was heavy on the north side, the weather would be good. When the canoe was about five miles offshore, the sealers looked to the land, and if they saw a little valley of fog that was low, it also meant good weather. However, if the fog was high, a blow was coming. The hunters sailed out to sea twenty to thirty miles to reach the sleeping seals. When they drew near a sleeping seal, the sealer had to paddle very quietly so he would not wake it, so quietly, in fact, it was said that a good hunter "could hear a sleeping seal snore" (Pettitt 1950: 9). When the hunters were within thrity feet of the seals, they threw their spears.

Traditionally, all species of seals were hunted for their meat and oil, which is used like butter (Daugherty 1948–49). It was not until the fur trade began in the late 1700s that seals were hunted for their skins and the art of seal hunting became more prominent. By the early twentieth century so many countries were harvesting fur seals that an international agreement was signed between the United States, Great Britain, Russia, and Japan to protect the species. The agreement protected the rights of coastal tribes to continue pelagic sealing but with nonmotorized boats and without firearms. The dangers these restrictions posed led to the near-abandonment of this hunting practice by the 1930s (Pettitt 1950: 45).

An example of the dangers involved occurred in 1920, when a great storm struck unexpectedly while a number of men were seal hunting. Twenty sealers from LaPush and the lower Hoh River drowned in the storm, but six men, including "Doctor" Lester, were saved by the steamer *Multnomah*. The steamer picked up the hunters' canoe and took the survivors to San Francisco. Doctor Lester, after being hauled aboard the steamship, sang his *tamanawis* (spirit power) song and took credit for "arranging" the rescue (Pettitt 1950: 45). A local pioneer recalls the day of this incident.

When night came on the Hoh Reservation, the Indians became very worried and they stayed up almost all night. The next day they all watched from the beach and long into the next night. . . . They all watched for an empty canoe to come floating to shore. In about two weeks. . . . there was a telegram sent by the Red Cross from San Francisco; the ship landed there with the Indians and their canoe. The Red Cross sent them home, but the canoe was a total loss to them. There was a big celebration on the reservation when [they] arrived home. (Cited in Smith 1976: 59–60)

SETTLEMENT

The Hoh are a small tribe, but according to tradition, there were more people here before the arrival of the *hokwat'* (drifting people). With the European explorers came diseases previously unknown to the Hoh. In 1942 Hoh tribal member Frank Fisher recalled his childhood for a report on "usual and accustomed fishing grounds and stations." The author of the report recorded that when Fisher was a small boy in the 1870s "there were only about 50 members of the Hoh Indian tribe although he was told that long prior to that time there were many more but that they had died on account of the smallpox epidemic which killed almost all of the Indians of the tribe" (Swindell 1942: 185). We know from spoken history that many people died during a severe smallpox epidemic that struck soon after the first Europeans arrived (Swindell 1942: 224) and other epidemics followed. By 1901 an official census counted only sixty-four Hoh tribal members.

Known settlements and housing patterns of the old days have been studied in an attempt to determine the precontact tribal population. Historically, there were seven villages along the Hoh, where several nuclear families lived in shed-roofed longhouses. The tribal population has been estimated based on an average of ten inhabitants per house at the following sites:

1. Chala'kw, the village at the mouth of the river on the site of the present-day Lower Hoh River Reservation. It was "the main village" and may have had five houses.
2. Ciłet' (tsay-klay-it, meaning "water pushing rock"), located one-half mile upstream from the mouth of the river on the south bank.
3. C'ixiłayax (tse-qhilk-lay-ah-quah, meaning "high bank"), located a little below the precipitous riverbank, one-half mile above Braden Creek.
4. C'olop'oltal "end place *or* border place" (also recorded as Tohoe-poe-qwat, meaning "end of good country before bad country begins," because the journey from this point on was more difficult).

5. Xwatsiya'bidɬxʷ (*koatse-a-bi-dilkh*, meaning not known), located a mile and a half above T'solop'oltal.

6. Dowaka' (Due-whah-a-kah, based on the Quinault word for cow parsnip or Indian rhubarb), located across from the mouth of Owl Creek.

Theodore Hudson carving a canoe with his grandson. Photo by Ruth Kirk.

7. ɬa'wa'qɬaqʷ (*klow-wuk-klulkh*, meaning "other side of the sandbar"), located above Dowaka' at the mouth of a small unnamed creek. (Swindell 1942: 185–86).

Assuming that the village at the mouth of the river had five houses and each of the other six settlements had one house, a precontact population of 110 is realistic. This estimate does not include families that were known to have lived on Destruction Island or along the coast at other drainages (Daugherty 1948–49: 2:20; Swindell 1942: 186). There were also "a number of places further upstream which were used by the Hoh Indians . . . principally for hunting elk, bear and other game" (Swindell 1942: 186–87).

Traditional Hoh life was family oriented. Each extended family had an elder or family chief who was the final authority in group decisions. Political power, wealth, and status were acknowledged at a potlatch, a several-day-long family feast. At a name-giving potlatch, a child was given a traditional name and the associated prerogatives to songs, dances, and spirit powers. The family heads from each village and tribe were invited, fed, and given gifts for witnessing the public transfer of status from the original owner of the name to the children of the family.

According to various early statements recorded by the anthropologists Leo J. Frachtenberg (1916) and George A. Pettitt (1950: 4), "tribal" chieftains probably did not exist until they were appointed and commissioned by the treaty makers, although some family heads were wealthier and more powerful than others. The names of two Quileute and Hoh traditional leaders are now held by Hoh tribal members: Xawishat'a (Howeatl), primary signatory to the treaty, is held by David Rock Hudson; and Kilip, a form of the name *Kilapiⱬ* Chief Caleb, also a treaty signatory, is held by Daky Fisher.

SPOKEN HISTORY

Much of tribal history takes the form of spoken history, which the Hoh call *kixi'*. The Hoh River and the headlands along the beach were created by K'wati, who killed the chief of the wolves and then tried to escape from the other wolves. K'wati, Changer, made many of the animals, plants, and features of the physical environment.

The actions of the characters in these oral histories explain why things are as they are today. Bayak, Raven, is a trickster who stole the box in which a selfish man kept the sun disk and put it up in the sky. Pakwad, Skatefish, went up in the sky and is now the constellation known as the Big Dipper, but those stars appear to the Hoh as a diamond-shaped skate with a long curving tail. Taxwo'wo'ot, Rainbow, is a beautiful woman in a colored blanket.

Her husband had a yearning to wander, and Rainbow stretches up high, going here and there to look for him. KwokwolIsdo, Owl, is the only one of the large raptors that does not make his home on the South Fork of the Calawah. Owl moved away to live on the Hoh River because Pixt'adax, Eagle, was continuously bothering him to borrow his night-vision eyes (Eagle *did* borrow his eyes but returned them in such bad condition that he became Hohoh, Day-owl, because he could no longer see at night).

The Hoh's cultural narratives are often referred to as myths, which suggests that they are made-up stories. But the Hoh River people regularly encounter evidence of the truth in kixi' stories. T'ist'ilal, Thunderbird, is a good example of this. Old Thunderbird is probably the most famous of the story characters on the Hoh River. He lives in a den under the Blue Glacier below Mount Olympus and can still be heard roaring and thundering and shaking the earth. Thunderbird regularly catches whales, and while he is flying back to his lair with these gigantic creatures, he has dropped them and they have become great rocks. The Hoh River area has a number of *q*ʷ*al'ayaxi*, or whale rocks.

According to tradition, the Hoh, Quileute, and Chemakum came to be located where they are as a result of a flood caused by *T'ist'ilal* at the Time of Beginnings:

> Thunderbird was very angry one time. He caused the ocean to rise. When the water began to cover things, the Quileute [speakers] got into their boats. The waters rose for four days. They rose until the very tops of the mountains were covered with water. The Quileute in their boats sailed wherever the wind and the currents carried them. They had no way to direct themselves. There was no sun. There was no land. For four days the water receded. But now the people were much scattered. When they reached land, some of the people were at Hoh; so they lived there from that time on. Others landed at Chemakum and stayed there. Only a few succeeded in finding their way back to Quileute. (Reagan and Walters 1933: 322)

This story is connected to the history of the Hoh language, which is actually called Quileute, spoken by both the Hoh and the Quileute. It is one of two languages in the Chimakuan language family, the second being Chemakum, spoken by the Chemakum Tribe, who lived near Port Townsend. The Chemakum's numbers were so drastically reduced that they were absorbed into the S'Klallam, Skokomish, and other groups by the 1850s.

Although the flood story is quite specific regarding how the Hoh and Quileute are related, there are some unanswered questions about Hoh tribal history. In 1916, when the anthropologist Leo Frachtenberg was interviewing Hoh and Quileute elders, he wrote that the Hoh speak Quileute but that according to Arthur Howeattle, "the old, real Hohs are Quinault and only the younger generation speaks Quiliute [*sic*]"(Frachtenberg 1916: 2:4). It is probable that the Hoh became Quileute by marriage. According to the same source, the Quinault at Queets and Hoh used to obtain their wives from the Quileute, "and this went on until all the Hohs began to speak Quiliute [*sic*]" (Frachtenberg 1916: 2:9).

Similar recollections were told to other early anthropologists as well, which suggests that the original Hoh inhabitants spoke Quinault and over time became bilingual through intermarriage with Quileute speakers. The children of a couple with different mother tongues usually learned the languages of both parents.

Much of Hoh spoken history predates written history. However, a very interesting story relating to a Russian shipwreck and a crew who spent the winter on the upper Hoh River has been passed down in spoken history for almost two hundred years. This account was also documented by the Russian crew's second in command, Timofei Tarakanov, who had it written down on his return to New Archangel (Sitka)(Owens and Donnelly 1985: 5).

In 1808 the Russian schooner *Sv. Nikolai* ran aground north of the Quillayute River. The Russian account tells us that the Indians (Quileute) were pilfering items from the Russian camp. Communication between the groups was limited, and the Russians forced the Quileute from the encampment. The Quileute began to hurl rocks at the crew, and the Russians opened fire. In the ensuing battle, all of the Russians were injured from rocks and arrows and three Quileute were killed by gunfire (Owens and Donnelly 1985: 46).

The Russians fled south along the coast to the Hoh River, where about two hundred Indians, including Hoh, Quileute, and Quinault were waiting. Ben Hobucket, a Quileute, describes the encounter:

> The Hoh Indians had a village on the other side of the river, and from it Indians came over to take a look at the new people, appearing friendly. So the strangers got them to agree to ferry them across the stream. . . . The white people and their belongings were placed in several canoes and the Hohs started to paddle them over; but, on reaching the middle of the stream, they suddenly opened up lightly plugged holes in the bottom of the canoes which they had intentionally cut and stuffed with cedar bark. Then, leaping from the crafts, they swam ashore, for could they get the new people adrift they could capture them single-handed without much trouble. (Reagan 1934: 87)

Some of the Russian crew were taken captive, and others fled upriver, where they spent the winter trading with Hoh villagers for food. When the Hoh refused, the Russians were "forced to take strong measures" (Owens and Donnelly 1985: 53). After the winter the Russians surrendered at the mouth of the Hoh River. The surviving crew members were taken as slaves among the tribes along the coast and most ended up near Neah Bay (Owens and Donnelly 1985:59, 61). In spring 1810, Captain Brown of the U.S. ship *Lydia* bought back thirteen members of the Russian crew from the Makah and returned them to Sitka (Owens and Donnelly 1985).

The only other well-documented account of maritime explorers at the Hoh before the Russian visit was that of the British fur trader Charles William Barkley and his ship, the *Imperial Eagle*, in 1787. It has been written in subsequent history books that six crewmen were killed by the Hoh at the mouth of the river and that is how Destruction Island came to be named. However, Mattie (Wheeler) Howeattle, born on the Hoh River on April 2, 1861, was an enrolled Quinault who once told a reporter that "coastal Indians never massacred ship-wrecked sailors. . . . The Hoh River people never killed" and "turn their heads" when they see this story displayed on a sign at the overlook to Destruction Island (*Seattle Times* 1961). The sign has since been removed.

Other explorers may have visited this area occasionally. But it appears to have remained largely unaffected by events of the outside world until 1855. In February of that year territorial governor Isaac Stevens began negotiations for a treaty with representatives of the Queets, Quinault, Upper and Lower Chehalis, and other tribes, but negotiations were terminated unsuccessfully, because the Indians refused to leave their homeland. Stevens's notes from the meeting indicate that the Hoh and Quileute groups who spoke a different language were not represented, because Stevens had not known of their existence before the negotiations at Chehalis. The following July, the treaty was renegotiated with the Quinault and Queets, this time with the omission of the Chehalis and the addition of the Hoh and Quileute.

The treaty of 1855, known as the Treaty of Olympia, was ratified by Congress in 1859 and ceded a majority of the western Olympic Peninsula to the United States, stipulating the removal of the tribes to a reservation somewhere along the coast. The signatory leaders may not have understood the terms of the treaty, which was negotiated in Chinook Jargon, a trade language with a vocabulary of about five hundred words. When the reservation at Quinault was set aside in 1863, the Hoh refused to move there. In October 1872 Indian agent R. H. Milroy discussed the reasons the Hoh refused to leave their homes:

> The Quiliutes, Hohs, and Quits [*sic*] reside at different points and distances on the coast north of the [Quinault] reservation, and say they never agreed to sell their country, nor did they, to their knowledge, sign any treaty disposing of their right to it.... The paper that they signed was explained to them to be

Hoh village at the river mouth. Photo by Ruth Kirk.

an agreement to keep the peace with citizens of the United States, and to accord them the same rights to come into their country and trade for furs. . . . They therefore refuse to leave their homes and localities in which they then and still reside, and move on the reservation which they . . . regard as the homes and property of the Quinaielts [sic]. (ARCIA 1872: 339–40)

On September 11, 1893, President Grover Cleveland signed an executive order establishing the Hoh Reservation on the lower Hoh River. At about the same time, settlers began to enter the territory.

Reservation Community

Today the 443-acre Hoh Reservation is a modern but isolated native community. There are currently 186 Hoh tribal members, 94 of whom live on the reservation.

After the tribe incorporated in 1969, under the provisions of the Indian Reorganization Act, the Hoh constitution and bylaws provided for an elected tribal council of four members with two-year concurrent (rather than staggered) terms. Although there is an elected chairperson, the Hoh people still recognize their traditional leaders.

The tribe has a tribal police department, fisheries enforcement, a natural resources office, and various tribal social service units. There is no school on the reservation, so the children go to school in Forks or elsewhere.

The tribe's natural resources department employs fisheries, habitat, and water quality staff who work to protect the fish, wildlife, and water resources that provide habitat and fish and game for the future. The Hoh River is recognized as one of several significant rivers of origin for wild salmon runs, and therefore it is terribly important to protect the future balance of this fishery. The tribe is a co-manager with the Washington State fisheries department and determines escapement or harvest quotas through documentation of spawning salmon.

Tribal members working for the tribe's fishery division count the salmon nests (redds) for each run of salmon that return to the river throughout the year. They begin the cycle by counting the spring chinook, which enter the river in April and spawn in the early fall; this count is followed by the fall chinook, which spawn by November. Then the fall coho that enter the river in September and spawn in early winter are counted. The annual count is completed with the steelhead that enter the river system in November to spawn in the spring. The other two species of salmon, chum and sockeye, are also present in limited numbers. According to tribal elder Alvin Penn, in the past there were so many fish that they could be seen moving upriver in schools, finning and jumping as they swam. Timber harvest and related activities have contributed to a drastic reduction in the number of salmon returning to the Hoh watershed, which comprises federal, state, and private lands. The Hoh natural resources staff conducts research and enhancement projects and evaluates activities that affect fish habitat and water quality. The tribe works in partnership with landowners through the 1988 Timber, Fish, and Wildlife Agreement to address proposed activities that could harm the fisheries resource. The plant and animal life of the Hoh River has changed because previous management activities did not consider the larger ecosystem, where everything is interdependent, including Hoh lifeways.

The Hoh Tribe has always depended on the fisheries of this river. Given the tribe's limited land base and scarce economic opportunities, subsistence fishing and gathering remains the most important component of Hoh lifeways. Today, near the river's mouth, the fishermen tend their nets. When the smelt visit the shores, dip nets are used just as K'wati showed the Hoh when he transformed them from the *p'ip'isodac'iti* (upside-down people).

Heritage Programs

Quileute is one of the few languages in the world that has no "nasal"—*m* or *n*—sounds. Linguists have studied Quileute for more than three decades and have developed a language learning program on the Quileute Reservation. This curriculum is also used by Hoh youth. Unfortunately, today there are very few people remaining who speak the language fluently.

Some of the community still get together on the beach and play their *kaxʷil* (drums) and sing old songs. Elders tell stories about the old days or relate stories of K'wati, Bayak, and *Dask'iya*, the kelp-haired cannibal woman who carries children off to her camp and cooks them. A tribal member stands in the river in solitude and a song comes to him. As an eagle feather floats to his feet, he picks it up, proud of the power and strength it carries. At a gathering or celebration where gifts are distributed and presentations are made, the announcer concludes the event by stating:

> We are proud of our culture and determined that it will continue. For that is what makes us the Hoh. We're still here on our river, near the places where our chiefs' burial trees were located. We're still here and we'll always be here. *Tsosa'a!* So much for that!

Visitor Opportunities

The Hoh reservation is very small and does not have formal visitor facilities. The tribal center lobby contains a beautiful carving of Thunderbird and historic photographs of Hoh elders. Sometimes the tribe has shirts or hats depicting the Hoh tribal logo for sale here, and a few of the residents sell basketry from their homes.

There is access to the mouth of the Hoh River on either side. From the north side, via the Oil City Road to Olympic National Park, one can see the Hoh Reservation. The most special place on the Hoh Reservation is the river mouth and ocean. There is no development, only peace and serenity. Visitors are welcome.

SUGGESTED READING

Jefferson County Historical Society. 1966. *With Pride in Heritage: History of Jefferson County.* Portland, Ore.: Professional Publishing Printing.
Kirk, Ruth. 1967. *David, Young Chief of the Quileutes: An American Indian Today.* New York: Harcourt, Brace & World.
Owens, Kenneth N., and Alton S. Donnelly. 1985. *The Wreck of the "Sv. Nikolai."* Portland, Ore.: Western Imprints.

Tom Jackson, captain of *kʷǡᵂiya* en route to Bella Bella, 1993. Photo by
Chris Morganroth III.

Quileute

Chris Morganroth III

For the students of the Quileute Tribal School

Cultural History

The narrative accounts of Pacific Northwest peoples contain a great treasure. When Quileute narratives are brought together, we find a clear chronology of tribal history, which preserves the details of the Quileute people's relationship to the world around them. Quileute territory is drained by the Sol Duc, Calawah, Bogachiel, and Dickey Rivers, all of which join to form the Quillayute before it flows into the ocean at La Push, the village where most Quileute live today.

Stories tell of spirit beings and monsters from the Time of Beginnings that still live among the Quileute. These stories, passed down from the elders to the children of each succeeding generation, speak of the past, of the relationship between the people, other living things, and the land, and of the personal qualities of living things that are valued today. These stories are often referred to as "myth" or "legend," but to the Quileute they are a way to explain events in history. The story of the creation of Hot Springs is just one example.

Two monsters, one Quileute and one Elwha, met occasionally in massive combat at the boundary between Elwha and Quileute territory. Evenly matched, they laid waste to a vast area and wounded each other grievously, but neither ever killed the other. After the last such battle, both monsters limped home to their caves, walled themselves in, and cried over their wounds. The steaming hot tears of both have run out of their lairs and accumulated to make the Sol Duc and Olympic Hot Springs. The Quileute call the monster whose tears

make the Sol Duc Hot Springs a'latkit, "the monster who cries in the woods."
(Morgenroth 1991: 108).

Elders relate that the world was not created; it always existed. However, at
the Time of Beginnings, a Changer known as K'wati went around trans-
forming features of the landscape and living things into the forms they have
today. This Changer was short and bald and could conceal his identity so he
would not be recognized. He had the power and imagination to make the
world as wondrous as it is. K'wati made the rivers of the Olympics and the
features of the coastline while he was being chased around by wolves.
Carrying only a container of sea mammal oil and a comb, K'wati tried to
slow down and elude the wolves by dumping oil here and there, which
flowed downhill and turned into the rivers. He also used his comb to make
great divots in the beach sand, which grew into headlands so that the wolves
had to swim around them, which allowed the Changer to escape. Later
K'wati came back and near the mouth of the Quillayute River changed the
wolves into the ancestors of the Quileute. So the Quileute have lived here
since the Time of Beginnings.

The tribes along the coast sometimes quarreled and fought for little reason. Their differences were getting out of hand, which angered K'wati, whose
home was in the mountains. The Changer warned all the people that he was
going to cause a Great Flood and rid the land of the people if they could not
get along. Some people began to prepare for the rising water by building big
canoes and plaiting thick ropes of cedar bark. Not long after the cedar canoes
were completed, K'wati called up the warm chinook wind. These warm
winds (which still blow today but not as fiercely as when K'wati made them)
melted the snow and ice in the mountains. This caused high water in the
rivers, and the oceans rose as well. Soon the land was covered with water,
except for the peaks of the Olympics. The only ones who survived were those
who had taken the Changer's warnings seriously.

The Quileute floated in their great canoes to the dry mountaintops, where
canoes from other tribes and the animals had taken refuge. As the waters
began to recede, the Quileute canoes were cast up on the banks of the rivers
of Quileute country and along the coast at the mouth of the Quillayute
River, Jackson Creek, and elsewhere. That is why many Quileute families
lived at communities upriver while others lived on the coast.

One of the Quileute canoes had broken loose and its occupants lost their
paddles; without them they floated to the northeast corner of the peninsula,
and there they settled, becoming the Chemakum people who spoke a language like that of the Quileute. The Chemakum Tribe was largely decimated
by warring groups by the 1850s and had intermarried with the S'Klallam,

Skokomish, and other tribes. The last Chemakum speaker died in the 1940s. Thus the Quileute language is known as an isolate, or one that does not appear to be related to any other language in the world.

In July 1855 Indian agent Michael Simmons held a council on behalf of Governor Isaac Stevens with several Quileute headmen to discuss terms of a treaty. Among those who signed the treaty were Chief How-yat'l (Howiyatł); Tah-ah-ha-wht'l (Taxa'wił), who was next to the chief; and Kal-lape (Kalapi?), a powerful figure in Quileute history. The treaty provided that the Quileute would cede their traditional lands to the United States in return for an annual payment and a reservation somewhere in the area that would be shared with other tribes. In 1856 the Quileute leaders who had signed believed they had been misled, as they had not understood that signing the treaty would mean "selling" their traditional lands.

In 1879 Simmons returned to La Push with Indian agent Charles Willoughby to visit the chiefs and find out if they wanted to "remove to the Quinaielt Agency or remain at their old, ancestral homes, at La Push" (*Moore v. U.S.* 1946: 12). Notes from this meeting reveal that the Quileute would never have signed away their hunting grounds, fishing sites, or "the field where the camas grows" (*Moore v. U.S.* 1946: 13) if they had understood that these places were part of the cession. As a result, the agent suggested that the Quileute be given a reservation, which did not occur for another ten years.

In the early 1870s settlers began to arrive in Quileute territory. Shortly thereafter a fur-buying station was established near the mouth of the river, and trade goods became available to the Quileute. In 1883 A. W. Smith was sent to La Push as the first schoolteacher and Indian agent. Smith gave individual Quileute children names from American history (William Penn, Grover Cleveland, George Washington, Robert E. Lee); from his own family (Bright and Pullen); from Indian agents (Ward); and from other settlers (Taylor, Martin). Many of the settlers filed homestead claims on land that included upriver homesites and settlements, displacing Quileute families to villages at the river mouths.

In 1889 approximately one square mile at the mouth of the Quillayute River was set aside as a reservation by executive order of President Grover Cleveland. Shortly afterward the twenty-five longhouses at La Push were burned down while the Quileute were at Puget Sound picking hops. They returned to discover that their village had been razed, plowed, and sown in grass and that Dan Pullen, the factor at the trading post, had filed a homestead claim on the site. Pullen's claim was denied, but the Quileute had lost most of their traditional implements, tools, artwork, and ceremonial gear in the fire. The Quileute rebuilt their village with frame houses, rather than traditional longhouses, on government-surveyed lots.

La Push. Courtesy of North Olympic Library, Kellogg Collection.

TRADITIONAL RELIGIOUS BELIEFS AND SUBSISTENCE

From the earliest times, the Quileute have used the Quillayute River drainage area for homesites, fishing and hunting, root digging and berrying, and gathering plant material for medicine and manufacture, as well as for recreation and ceremonies.

Animals are vital to Quileute subsistence and figure importantly in the traditional worldview. Traditional beliefs put animals and people in the same natural hierarchy. Living things were divided into three categories: spirit beings, beings-with-souls, and other growing things.

Quileute ancestors felt that most living things had souls and fell into the beings-with-souls category: animals great and small, birds and fish, the great trees (but not small ones), Fog and the great rocks that are transformed creatures, Rainbow, some mountains, and, of course, the people. At the Time of Beginnings, the ancestors of all these beings-with-souls were creatures that could communicate with each other. They were later transformed by K'wati to have their own characteristics. For instance, sharp-eyed mole loaned his eyes to the originally nearsighted eagle, who never got around to returning them. Gray whales, wrens, skatefish, ravens, deer, and beaver were all First Beings that were transformed. Thus beings-with-souls are called *ixwat'so'*, meaning "changed things" in Quileute.

Some beings-with-souls were thought to be in a special, spiritually privileged subset because they travel in two natural elements: the powerful frog and otter live on land and in water; the raven lives in the air and on the ground; and the diving kingfisher lives in the air and under the water. Wolf belongs in this group because it was thought that when wolves leap into the ocean, they change into killer whales. Also included are Blue Jay, Rainbow, Mole, and Fog, who exist on the overlapping edges of the physical and spiritual world and serve as conduits between a person and his or her guardian spirit. They would appear to give a message from the spirit world such as "Your spirit power is happy or unhappy with you" or "Pay attention because something momentous is about to transpire."

Some creatures, especially otter and mole, could be conjured with when the mood was right, allowing someone who was in a right relationship with their spirit power to visualize where elk were to be found or to find a lost relative. Thus a person's medicine bag might contain a bone, a tooth, or a claw that had manifested itself at an auspicious time or that was known to be the thing that served as a conduit to the guardian spirit.

All animals were guided by the spirit world. So elk and deer and other game submitted themselves to those hunters who had the strongest spirit powers and who belonged to families that had not broken taboos. Animals were vital to traditional Quileute not only for the meat, hide, bone, antler, and sinew that the people needed but also because they were a contact point with the spiritual elements of the world. Some of these beliefs are still held by individual Quileute.

People and animals were much more alike at the Time of Beginnings, when they were called First Beings, before K'wati began to give them their own characteristics. For instance, he made Beaver into the first beaver by putting a mussel shell knife on his backside and made Deer into the ancestor of all deer by putting sharpened shell knives on the sides of his head for ears. The Quileute exemplify this process of transformation, having descended as a people from wolves who were changed by K'wati into the ancestors of the present-day Quileute.

In many other cultural narratives, animals were created from people. The Quileute, however, changed from animals into people. The old people believed that all of the First Beings had features of both people and animals. It is basic to the Quileute perspective that people are not higher or more special than other living things. It was a matter of concern that the Quileute were themselves beings-with-souls yet hunted and killed other beings-with-souls. And for that reason hunting was a pursuit that required sensitivity and ritual.

The Quileute relied equally on hunting and fishing until about 1900. At that time settlement and enforcement of state regulations forced the tribe to discontinue its established hunting practices on which their diet and mode of life depended. In 1916 Billy Hebaladup and Arthur Howeattle said, "In former days hunting was as important among us Quileutes as fishing" (Frachtenberg 1916: 3:37).

June was the most important hunting season, as by that time the bull elks had fattened in the upland areas. Several families hunted together. Although a good Quileute archer could shoot an arrow more than one hundred yards with accuracy, Quileute runners normally chased animals with dogs to killing zones near camp where the rest of the party hid in ambush along the trail. Elk cows were hunted in July and August, after rutting, when they were at peak fatness.

Deer were usually hunted on prairies (from June to September at dawn or twilight) and were not chased but shot from blinds and hiding places. Throughout the year, other mammals such as cougars, lynx, bear, raccoons, beaver, rabbits, grouse, eagles, seagulls, geese, ducks, and loons were hunted. The wolf, an ancestor of the Quileute, was not hunted.

Sea mammals such as fur and hair seals, sea lions, sea otters, porpoises, and whales were also hunted. All hunters belonged to spirit societies, and the whalers' society (called the oily voiced society) was the most prestigious. At times a whale-hunting crew spent long hours, days, or even weeks waiting for the harpooner, who was the leader, to prepare for the hunt. The harpooner had to go through a spiritual cleansing process that required bathing in the cold ocean water and talking to the spirit of the whale by singing a special song. When the harpooner felt that his body and soul were physically and spiritually clean, the hunt could begin. After the harpooned whale was subdued, buoys were secured to the carcass and the mouth was tied shut to prevent water from entering the whale and sinking it. Then the arduous task of towing it home began. Once the whale was beached, the meat was divided according to rank, with the chief and other leaders getting the choicest parts. Nothing was wasted.

Seal hunting was less strenuous, with only three men to a crew, whereas whale hunting required a crew of eight. Both kinds of hunting involved taboos. For example, you could not point with your index finger when you spotted a seal. If you did so, the seal would feel the point of your finger and escape. The spotter pointed with his thumb. The seal hunter's wife had to lie still in bed until the hunt was over, because the seal would do whatever the harpooner's wife did. If the wife lay unmoving, the seals would do the same thing. If a seal hunting crew came home empty-handed, a wife might be blamed for their lack of success. Whaling ceased for the Quileute in about 1900, and traditional seal hunting ended at the beginning of World War II. Today Quileute tribal members can obtain a permit from the Quileute Natural Resources Department to harvest a seal or sea lion for subsistence or ceremonial purposes. The Marine Mammal Protection Act "does not in any way diminish or abrogate existing protected Indian treaty fishing or hunting rights" (Marine Mammal Protection Act 1995: 17). It is up to the individual tribe to develop regulations regarding tribal marine mammal take.

For the Quileute, fish have always been a basic commodity of life. Fishing was continuous throughout the year, but the best seasons were March to May

Drawing of seal hunters by Dorothy Gurerro, Quileute Tribe.

and August to October. During those peak seasons, the families living at the mouth of the river would visit related families at fishing stations and settlements upriver.

The preferred method of fishing was the fish trap, a barricade of hemlock, vine maple, and willow poles stretched across the river with one or more platform-covered openings that migrating fish were channeled through into the scoop nets of waiting fishermen. Although fish traps belonged to the families that owned the village site, other families, by invitation, had access to use. Family groups from elsewhere were always able to secure use of a platform by giving a gift to the owner of the trap.

People who lived at settlements along the rivers invited those from downriver to fish and trade their elk, deer, and fish with Quileute who lived at the river mouth for dried sea mammal meat (and oil), smoked smelts, dried halibut, and rockfish, and dried clams and other mollusks. Arthur Howeattle said that upriver Quileute sometimes went a whole year without visiting La Push, but it was probably more common for families to maintain dwellings and subsistence routines both at the mouth of the river and at riverine villages.

September was hop-picking time. Since the 1880s the Quileute had traveled to the Tacoma area to camp, work hard in the hop harvest, sing, gamble, and socialize with other tribes. Then they would return for the silver and king salmon runs on the Quillayute River and resume the cycle in November.

Slowly, the pattern of fishing on the river changed, as the commercial gill net fishing industry developed and prospered. As early as 1912 the Quileute had to contest their rights under the treaty to fish in "usual and accustomed places." The importance of salmon in Quileute life is demonstrated by the continuing observance of the First Salmon ritual, which requires that the bones from the first fish of the season be returned to the river. Fish are a traditional and contemporary key resource for the Quileute.

Mussels, clams, chitons, and other tidal life were collected at a number of saltwater beach sites. These were eaten fresh, wind dried, or smoke dried. Some families had the right to exclusive use of particular beaches. These rights had to be publicly claimed at potlatches and validated by regular gifting of family leaders at ceremonies.

Old-time Quileute foraged for, collected, and used a wide variety of terrestrial plants, including trees. Because some growing things were only briefly available in season, the old people maintained patterns of movement that made certain they were in the right places at the right times. Families sometimes went to camp in rich foraging areas, and groups of women often followed trails to gathering places miles from home. The prairies, notably the Tyee and Beaver, Forks, Little Quillayute, and Quillayute, were basic to Quileute foraging patterns. However, there were also smaller maintained prairie areas near the Sol Duc Hot Springs, Shuwah, and upper Maxfield Creek. The prairies were maintained by regular burning to regenerate roots and berries of various kinds and browse that drew animals.

Luke Hobucket told how the prairies were created in an ongoing battle between Thunderbird and Killer Whale:

> The battle between them was terrible. The noise that Thunderbird made when he flapped his wings shook the mountains. They stripped the timber there. They tore the trees out by their roots. Ten Mimlos-whale got away.[1] Again Thunderbird caught Mimlos-whale. Again they fought a terrible battle in another place. All the trees there were torn out by their roots. Again Mimlos-whale escaped.
>
> Many times they fought thus. Each time Thunderbird caught Mimlos-whale there was a terrible battle, and all the trees in that place were uprooted. At last Mimlos-whale escaped to the deep ocean, and Thunderbird gave up the fight. That is why killer whale still lives in the ocean today. In those places where Thunderbird and Mimlos-whale fought, to this day, no trees grow. Those places are the prairies on the Olympic Peninsula today. (Quoted in Reagan and Walters 1933: 321)

When families camped on the prairies, they built three-sided huts of hemlock bark or shacks with roof and walls made of mats. Much of a woman's time was spent digging roots of various kinds that provided the small but important carbohydrate content of the aboriginal Quileute diet: primarily fern (brake, sword, licorice, wood), clover, silverweed, horsetail, wild parsnip, thistle, and tiger lily.

The primary root staples were camas and the rhizome of the brake fern, which was collected in quantity and then ground into a paste that was buried under the fire and baked into a breadlike loaf. This part of the diet was almost immediately replaced when potatoes, turnips, and carrots could be acquired from settlers and the La Push gardens were established after the school came in the 1880s. Albert Reagan (1934a: 57), schoolmaster there in 1905, reported that he had missed "fern-paste bread," since they had stopped using it by the time he arrived.

Although longtime use of fire to maintain the prairies is certain, the ethnographic record is not clear regarding the details of traditional burning strategies. Reagan (1934a: 56–57) does not tell what time of year the prairies were burned but writes, "The burning of [the bracken] fern year by year was what kept up the prairies. . . . The Indians burned the ferns for the purpose of clearing out the prairies so they could shoot the deer and elk when they came to feed on the young fern fronds." Ram Singh (1966: 43) mentions a family that "burned over its part of the prairie in the spring so that dead ferns would be destroyed, giving way to camas." Hal George remembered that the prairies were burned in *t'sakit'sa* (early September), when families had already foraged for roots and berries and the grasses were dry (Powell field notes 1978).

People eagerly collected spring sprouts (e.g., salmonberry, thimbleberry, cow parsnips, giant horsetail) and berries as they became ripe. Besides cakes of dried salal and huckleberries, a notable part of the Quileute diet was cooked red elderberries, prepared and stored for winter by baking the berries under a covering of skunk cabbage leaves and then storing the cooked berries in bark containers buried in sandy streambeds.

Grasses (bear grass, dune wild rye, and rye grass), "swamp grass" (slough sedge, *Carex obnupta*), reeds (tule and cattail), bark (cedar, wild cherry), and roots (e.g., spruce) were collected for basket weaving and mat making. Nearly every plant in the natural environment was used in some way in the complex traditional Quileute pharmacopoeia.

The western red cedar was of primary importance and continues to be important today. The large-girth tree and its bark were used for a wide variety of necessities in Quileute life and technology. Cedar splits easily and preserves well, so it was the perfect wood for house planks, support posts, canoes, and ceremonial objects. The cedar withes and inner bark were made into numerous items, such as towels, clothing, bedding, and baskets. For the Quileute, yellow cedar, hemlock, fir, vine maple, spruce, yew, and ocean spray (ironwood) were also basic to technology.

Contemporary Quileute Life

Today the Quileute Tribe has 723 members, about 400 of whom live at La Push. The tribe has its own law enforcement and court system, a health clinic, and the Quileute Tribal School for grades K–12 (including curriculum in the Quileute language and culture). The Shaker religion is still practiced, and there is also an Assembly of God church in the village.

Basket weaver Elsa Payne. Cattail in foreground. Quileute Tribe.

Quileute canoe makers in 1945. Quileute Tribe.

Laven Coe using D-adze on a canoe, 1947. Quileute Tribe.

TABLE 1. The 13 "moons" of the Quileute annual cycle. The Quileute moons do not coincide with the Julian calendar. Peoples on the coast had different names for the moons than people upriver; for example, March was called *yashabalktiya'at*, "fur seal hunting days."

Quileute Annual Cycle	Upriver Activities	Saltwater Activities
Kwawiya'aliktiya'at' "Steelhead-getting days" (approx. January)	Small mammal hunting, Steelhead fishing, fern and root gathering	Mollusk gathering
Libic'haspa "Main steelhead spawning time" (approx. February)	Steelhead fishing	Winter whale hunting
Xitsxits'aliktiya'at' "Skunk cabbage getting days" (approx. March)	Skunk cabbage and spring shoot gathering	Mussel and clam gathering, fur seals and sea lion hunting
Yacht'siyasiktiya'at'sa "salmonberry sprout days" (approx. April)	Camas, salmonberry, thimble-berry, and horsetail sprout gathering	Smelt (Hoh), cod, sea bass, halibut, and octopus fishing, clam harvesting
Bixaliktiya'at "flowers days" (approx. May)	Bird hunting, cedar bark collecting, spring (chinook) salmon and sockeye (blueback) fishing	Migratory bird hunting, fur seal and gray whale hunting
Cha'alowasiktiya'at "Salmonberry days" (approx. June)	Labrador tea and herb, clover root, camas, salmonberry, bird eggs, thimbleberry, and strawberry gathering	Smelt (LaPush) fishing, bird egg gathering
T'lax'aliktiya'at "elderberry getting days" (approx. July)	Trout, red huckleberry, bear, blueberry, elk & deer, currant, marmot, various blackberries	Hair seal hunting
Kwo'od'aliktiya'at "salalberry getting days" (approx. August)	Racoon hunting; red elder-berry, fern root, gooseberry, nettle fiber, salalberry (prairie burning), and crabapple gathering	Halibut fishing
T'sak'it'sa "no berries left time" (approx. early September)	Bear grass, cranberry, summer coho fishing, rosehip, and swamp grass gathering, elk and deer hunting	Shore grass
Sat'so'aliktiya'at "King salmon getting days" (approx. late September)	Cattail gathering, humpie salmon and king salmon fishing	
Ilaksi'aliktiya'at "Silver salmon getting days" (approx. October)	Olympic coho (silver) fishing, bear hunting	
T'lokwo'oktiya'at "Pond freeze days" (approx. November)	Beaver and land otter hunting, steelhead fishing	
Bask'alidix "Bad weather time" (approx. December)	Manufacture and repair (e.g., canoes, mats, baskets, nets), rituals, potlatch feasts, trade	

SOURCE: Powell, et al. 1995.

On July 24, 1937, the Quileute voted to accept the Indian Reorganization Act, and the secretary of the interior issued the *Corporate Charter of the Quileute Indian Tribe.* The Quileute constitution calls for a tribal council of five who are elected to staggered three-year terms. Although there is an elected tribal chairperson, the tribe continues to acknowledge its hereditary chiefs, and these titles are passed on through traditional ceremonies from generation to generation. The tribal council is the executive body of the tribe and is supported by various programs, including finance, natural resources, law enforcement, utilities, social services, and other administrative units.

Heritage Programs

Nearly all of Quileute culture and tradition is still part of daily life for the tribe, although few people speak the Quileute language fluently. Tribal members continue to make baskets from cedar bark and grasses. And canoes are carved as they were one hundred years ago. The Quileute participate in canoe journeys along the coast and Puget Sound with other tribes of the region.

In 1997 the Quileute hosted the annual canoe paddle journey to La Push. Eighteen tribal canoes from all over the Pacific Northwest, including Canada and southeastern Alaska, met at the `aká-lát event, meaning "top of the rock," for the island at the mouth of the Quillayute River. The island is also known as James Island, and it was a refuge for the Quileute people during times of war. Here they established a somewhat permanent lifestyle during the years of warfare. Gardens were raised and fruit trees were planted. Today the fruit trees still stand in testimony to former times.

Quileute paddlers. Photo by Chris Morganroth III.

àká-lát, or James Island, named in honor of Chief Jimmy Howe. Courtesy North Olympic Library, Kellogg Collection.

Visitor Opportunities

The beauty of the Quileute's natural environment is an attraction to people from around the world. Thousands visit the reservation and its beaches annually.

The reservation has hotel and cabin accommodations, as well as tent sites at the La Push Ocean Park Resort on First Beach. Visitor conveniences include a tribal store with artwork for sale, a grocery store, a gas station, and the Quileute Seafood Company, which sells fresh tribal catches of salmon, crab, and other delicacies in season and has a new café.

First Beach is a beautiful sandy crescent-shaped beach, popular for surfing, sea kayaking, and whale watching. Second Beach, in Olympic National Park, can be accessed from the parking lot in the reservation and is a short 0.6-mile hike. The historic Coast Guard station at La Push is a lovely building, which now houses tribal school operations.

The tribe is planning to build a museum soon to house their basketry and other collections and provide an opportunity for visitors to see canoe carvers and traditional celebrations.

Quileute Days is held the third weekend of July and includes a salmon bake, games, traditional dancing, sports contests, and loads of energy and fun.

Traditional-style salmon bake. Photo by Chris Morganroth III.

NOTES

1. The word Mimlos derives from the Chinook Jargon word *Mem'-a-loose* (dead, to die) correlating to "kill" and, in this case, "Killer" Whale.

SUGGESTED READING

Pettit, George A. 1950. "The Quileute of La Push: 1775-1945." *Anthropological Records*. 14: 1.

Powell, J. V., and Vickie Jensen, 1976. *Quileute: An Introduction to the Indians of La Push*. Seattle: University of Washington Press.

Reagan, Albert B., and L. V. W. Walters. 1933. "Tales from the Hoh and Quileute." *Journal of American Folklore* 46 (182): 297–346.

The Mussel Gatherer, by Edward S. Curtis, 1900. Intertidal seafood filled cedar bough and spruce root burden baskets, a common sight along the coast. Today the Makah continue to harvest traditional foods. Courtesy of MSCUA, University of Washington Libraries, NA322.

Makah

Melissa Peterson and the
Makah Cultural and Research Center

NATION

biʔidʔa , di·ya·, waʔač̓, c̓u·yas, ʔuse·ʔit

Makah spoken history tells the story of ancient times when the Makah people, the *qʷidičča?a·tx*,[1] lived in a world that revolved around the sea and land. Yet it never lets one forget the great cultural changes that brought the tribe to where it is today, a sovereign nation in its traditional homeland. Makah tribal members live both on the reservation and throughout the world practicing an intertwined contemporary and native culture. The Makah, both past and present, have demonstrated their ability to adapt, survive, and flourish.

Cultural History

TRADITIONAL MAKAH TERRITORY

In the days before sustained contact with Europeans, the Makah lived in five permanent villages in their homeland. Bordered by the waters of the Strait of Juan de Fuca on the north and the Pacific Ocean on the west, Makah territory encompassed an extensive coastal and inland area. The Makah used many fishing, whaling, and seal hunting grounds in their traditional sea territory, which extended south near Cape Johnson, north to 40-Mile Bank, and east to the Lyre River on the Strait of Juan de Fuca. Some resource acquisition areas were shared with the Quileute to the south and the S'Klallam to the east. The Sooes, Waatch, Hoko, Ozette, Big, Sekiu, Pysht, Lyre, and Twin Rivers were Makah fishing locations. Lake Ozette, Hobuck Lake, and Elk Lake were also important for fishing and gathering. Makah lands encompassed the islands of Waadah, Tatoosh, Ozette, Cannon Ball, the Bodeltas, and islands on Lake Ozette. All of these places have meaningful Makah names that continue to be important to tribal lifeways. It is difficult to determine exactly how far out to sea the Makah traveled; however, it is known that they traveled well out of sight of land.

The Makah had many summer and permanent villages within their vast territory. Five large permanent villages located along the shore of the most northwestern point in the contiguous United States are known as *biʔidʔa* (Bahaada), *diˑyaˑ* (Deah), *waʔač,* (Waatch), *čuˑyas,* (Sooes), and *ʔuseˑʔił* (Ozette). In the early 1800s, before epidemics, these villages were home to between two thousand and four thousand people. Each village contained several cedar plank longhouses, approximately 30 feet wide and 70 feet long.

Extended families lived in the longhouses, and it was common to have several generations under one roof. During the summer months, people traveled to various summer residences, such as Kidickabit, Archawat, Hoko, Tatoosh Island, Ozette River, and Ozette Lake. The summer camps were closer to fishing, whaling, and gathering areas.

Photo of Deah (Neah Bay), one of the five permanent villages of the Makah, in the early 1900s. Neah Bay is now the central village for most Makah residents. This photograph captures an early transitional period in the Makah lifestyle. Canoes line the beach, although European-style homes have replaced the traditional longhouse. Photo by E. S. Meany, Makah Cultural and Research Center.

Photo of a whale being butchered on the beach, early 1900s. Whale processing was performed by people who specialized in this field. Tradition demanded an in-depth understanding of butchering techniques and the social protocol for distribution. Photo by Samuel G. Morse, Makah Cultural and Research Center.

The Makah had a keen understanding of and great respect for their environment, which sustained them through the wet, dark, cold coastal winters. As people oriented to the seasons, they knew when and where to hunt or gather food and materials in balance with life cycles. They observed the cultural tradition of using nearly all of what was taken from the land and the sea.

The Makah possessed highly sophisticated navigational and maritime skills that enabled them to travel on the rough Pacific Ocean and the swift water of the Strait of Juan de Fuca. They used various sizes of oceangoing canoes made from western red cedar. Salmon fishing canoes, halibut, whaling, sealing, and war canoes, as well as large cargo canoes, were owned by tribal members. The canoes had sails to take advantage of windy conditions. They were landed on the beach, stern first, in case the paddlers needed to leave quickly. The canoes were never disturbed, as respect for another's belongings was ingrained in every person. The Makah were expert canoeists and would travel great distances to obtain food or trade their wealth.

Various fish and marine mammals were main staples to the Makah people. Halibut and salmon were caught, smoked, or sun dried and stored in large quantities for winter consumption, and varieties of bottomfish were caught year-round. Porpoise and fur and harbor seals were eaten fresh or smoked and the sealskins were cured and used for floats. Seal blubber was rendered into valuable food oil, which was used at every meal. Even the entrails were used to make rope or containers for liquids. Sea otters were a highly valued trade item. The sale of sea otter skins in the 1700s could earn the seller enough to purchase a schooner. The otter skin was also made into a chafe guard on capes and cedar clothing.

Whales were hunted for their meat and blubber, and nearly every part was used. Among the species hunted were the humpback, gray, right, sperm, fin, and blue whale. Oil rendered from whale blubber was an important food product and a valuable trading commodity up and down the coast. The oil was purchased by the Hudson's Bay Company in Victoria and was used locally to lubricate machinery and in oil lamps (Lane 1973: 17). The bones of the whale were used to make combs, spindle whorls, bark pounders and shredders, D-adz handles, war clubs, and adornment. While the sea provided an abundance of good things to eat, the rocky coast held other feasts.

The intertidal zone offered a large variety of nutritious and tasty foods: several different types of clams and snails, mussels, chitons, sea roses, sea urchins, barnacles, and crabs. Seaweed was gathered and eaten, and seabirds such as ducks were hunted for food and used in clothing.

The shell of the mussel was sanded, shaped, and sharpened into various blades for implements. Dentalium, another important shell, was a prized trading commodity; strands of the shell were used like money. Dentalium regalia, such as breastplates and headpieces, were used in puberty ceremonies and as a sign of wealth. This regalia continues to be passed down from generation to generation. Harvesting the dentalium was a specialized skill that required a sophisticated retrieval tool.

Land animals, including deer, elk, beaver, bear, rabbit, and fowl, were hunted and trapped. Like the marine mammals, their bones were used for a variety of implements and their skins were used for clothing, drums, or dance gear.

To maintain a well-rounded diet, the Makah gathered plants, bulbs, and berries that they ate fresh or preserved for winter use. For medicinal purposes, leaves, flowers, bark, and roots were gathered, preserved, and stored as well.

There were several different ways to prepare food. Some food, like sprouts, tubers, chitons, and sea urchins, were eaten raw. Halibut, salmon, and duck were roasted or baked over or under hot coals. Bottomfish, salmon, seal, whale, deer, and duck were boiled by adding hot rocks to water in bentwood boxes or were steamed in a pit. By smoking and sun drying foods like halibut and salmon, the Makah preserved their resources for the winter.

A 300- to 500-year-old western redcedar carved to represent a whale saddle and elaborately inlaid with otter teeth. Western redcedar was carved into objects of art, split and planked for longhouses, and hewn and carved into canoes and other functional items. This representation of the whale's saddle, the tastiest part of the whale's meat, represents ceremonial whaling traditions. Makah Cultural and Research Center.

The Makah had an in-depth understanding of wood technology. They manufactured tools, gear, and household items from the root, bark, wood, and bough of the spruce, hemlock, cedar, alder, maple, crabapple, wild cherry, and yew. This enabled them to make everything they needed to survive on the land and sea.

A tree that was used in its entirety was the western red cedar. All parts of the cedar were used to make utilitarian items. The bark was either split, shredded, pounded, or twisted to make mats, hats, cradle boards, pouches, clothing, rope, and many styles of baskets and containers. Cedar boughs and roots were strong and used for ropes and baskets. The wood was split into boards for house planks, bentwood boxes, and masks. Whole timbers were peeled and meticulously adzed to become frames for buildings. Cedar logs were split in half, hewn, steamed, and fashioned into various types of canoes.

The Makah's social structure enabled them to organize the various duties of gathering food, making clothing, building homes, and raising children as well as maintaining order and etiquette among themselves and with their neighbors. The Makah classes, chieftain, commoner, and slave, established a specific hierarchy of duties and responsibilities. Strictly enforced arranged marriages within the same class assured continuity of this system.

The chieftain position was generally inherited by the firstborn male through the father's lineage. In the event of a death or an unsuitable heir, another family member was selected and groomed for the position.

A chief was expected to possess certain social qualities, such as honesty, generosity, compassion, diplomacy, and integrity. He also had to be from a whale hunting family. From birth, he received training from both the men and the women in his family. Members of his family were also trained to conduct themselves properly. The well-being of the tribe was not solely dependent on the chief, however.

Secret societies upheld social values and compliance with established rules. The entire tribe had to adhere to social rules or face often-harsh consequences. Positions within a society were inherited, and initiation took place in ceremonies held during the winter. Song and dance accompanied the rituals at village gatherings.

Another important aspect of Makah life was the potlatch, which enhanced social standing and redistributed wealth and property. Potlatches were social events that marked passages in life, recorded oral history, and maintained the status of families. Marriage and naming ceremonies, coming-of-age parties, memorials, and feasts would sometimes last up to ten days, and neighboring tribes were invited. There was a strict protocol in the organization and presentation of the event, where family and guests reiterated their family privileges and entertained each other with inherited songs and dances and elaborate ceremonies commemorating the event. Preparation for these great feasts might take years, as the family needed to acquire enough gifts to distribute to all the guests. While the potlatch was an integral part of the culture, family was the fabric of Makah society.

The Makah were generous hosts, but they were also fierce warriors. They did not tolerate abuses from other tribes and defended themselves and their territory against raiders and war parties. They often took the heads of their enemies and placed them on poles as a warning to others. Kinship ties with other groups facilitated alliances in times of war. They were also important for status and connections to specific resources. They were highly regarded and respected, and people were taught both their maternal and paternal family origin, which included relations to other tribes. For example, the Makah are closely related to the Nuu-chah-nulth on Vancouver Island. This connection must be a very ancient one, as their languages are both in the Wakashan language family and Nootkan subgroup. The two nations frequently crossed the strait to visit each other and had boundary agreements before Washington Territory was established. The Makah and the Nuu-chah-nulth assisted each other in time of war and celebrated potlatches. Today potlatches and cultural events are held by both to show respect for this long-standing relationship.

Respectful behavior, which contributed to family solidarity, was instilled from very early in life. Children were highly regarded, and great care was taken to assure their physical, spiritual, and emotional well-being. Women had responsibility for ensuring the wellness of their offspring: they observed rules for prenatal care that protected the fetus from harm. For example, a pregnant woman was not to look at an octopus, because it was so ugly it might have an effect on the baby's development. She also had a wealth of knowledge of medicinal herbs to keep her healthy in pregnancy and ease childbirth. All tribal members cherished infants and children and taught them a sense of belonging and value. Stories and legends, an integral part of the tribe's lifestyle, were told to demonstrate how to conduct oneself in the family and the community. Grandparents, aunts, and uncles were key people in the upbringing of small children.

TRANSITIONAL MAKAH LIFE

Makah society began to change with the coming of introduced diseases and foreign ideologies. By the late 1700s indirect contact with Europeans had a devastating effect on the Makah people. Thousands died from smallpox epidemics, tuberculosis, influenza, and whooping cough. The deaths disrupted the sharing of traditional knowledge and left large gaps in the transfer of Makah culture. Some cultural knowledge was never recovered, but some has been reclaimed through the years. During the epidemics, people suffered unfathomable grief, fear, and confusion, which may explain why recovery was difficult. Successive bouts of smallpox tragically reduced the southernmost villages in 1852, striking just a few years before the signing of the treaty of Neah Bay.

On January 31, 1855, the Makah villages were represented by forty-two Makah dignitaries to negotiate and sign a treaty between the United States and the Makah Indians. Negotiations between Gov. Isaac Stevens and tribal representatives were held at Neah Bay in Chinook Jargon, with English interpreters. The Makah tribal forefathers protected whaling, fishing, sealing, and village land rights from annihilation. Certain rights were specifically outlined in the articles of the treaty to ensure that the importance of continuing these

Elder Helma Ward telling stories to children. The age-old art of storytelling continues today. Storytelling was and continues to be intertwined in everyday life as a source of entertainment as well as education. Photo by Theresa Parker, Makah Cultural and Research Center.

traditional practices was clearly understood. The tribe sacrificed, or ceded title to, 300,000 acres of Makah territory, and in exchange, a relationship with the federal government was established to protect the health, education, and welfare of the Makah. In 1859 Congress ratified the treaty; this event signified the beginning of radical cultural changes imposed on the Makah by federal polices and the people who implemented them.

Representatives of the U.S. government—Indian agents, missionaries, and schoolteachers—enforced assimilation policies and laws. Although many measures were taken to thwart Makah culture, such as prohibiting the potlatch, ceremonial passages, and the Makah language, the Makah people resisted. The resistance against completely conforming to Euro-American standards is reflected in the continuance of Makah culture today.

Contemporary Makah Life

Since the signing of the treaty more than one hundred forty years ago, there have been many changes to the Makah way of life. As it was with tribal ancestors before contact, the land and sea continue to be important to the $q^w idičča\mathrm{?}a\cdot tx$ people. Makah territory has increased since the establishment

of the Makah Reservation under the Treaty of Neah Bay. The initial reservation was expanded in 1872 and 1873.

The population of the 719-acre Ozette Reservation, set aside by executive
order in 1893, was greatly reduced in 1896 when most families moved to
Neah Bay after the government mandated that their children must attend
school. By the 1930s the last remaining Ozette had left, and the federal government discussed the disposition of the reservation lands. On October 22,
1970, the Ozette Reservation was returned to the Makah Tribe. In 1984
Congress returned Tatoosh and Wa-ada Islands to the tribe. Makah territory
has also increased by the outright purchase of several thousand acres, making the reservation forty-seven square miles or 30,142 acres.

After years of state restrictions on tribal fishing rights, on February 12,
1974, the tribe's "usual and accustomed" fishing "grounds and stations" on
land and sea were defined by a federal court. Extensive research into the oral
and physical forms of Makah history led Judge George Boldt to conclude,

> The Makah's usual and accustomed fishing places prior to treaty time
> included the waters of the Strait of Juan de Fuca to Port Crescent (near Port
> Angeles) extending out into the ocean to an area known as Swiftsure and then
> south along the Pacific Coast to an area intermediate to Ozette Village and the
> Quileute Reservation, as well as the rivers along the Strait of Juan de Fuca and
> down the Pacific shore starting at the Elwah [sic] River including the Lyre
> River, Twin River, Pysht River, Hoko River, Sekiu River, Sooes River, Waatch
> River, Big River, and Ozette River and Lake Ozette. (U.S. v. Washington, 384 F.
> Supp. 364)

These fishing areas continue to be as crucial to Makah culture and lifeways as they had been for their ancestors.

Neah Bay is the main village on the Makah Reservation. The word *Neah* is
derived from the old village named Deah, located on the western edge of the
current village of Neah Bay. The main village was located at this site for several reasons, one of the most significant being the requirement for children
to attend a school here during the late 1800s. Families moved to Neah Bay to
care for and be with their children. When the 1887 Allotment Act was implemented at Neah Bay between 1907 and 1912, the Makah people acquired
ten-acre parcels outside the village and homesites at Neah Bay. There are also
scattered residences at Waatch, Sooes, and Bahaada today.

The population of the Makah Reservation is approximately 1,800, including both Makah and non-Makah residents. According to tribal records, there
are 2,303 currently enrolled Makah tribal members, and of those 1,400 reside
on the reservation. An Indian Health Service unit provides medical and dental care for community members, but the nearest hospitals are more than an
hour away, in Forks and Port Angeles.

The last longhouse was torn down in about 1903, at the behest of the Indian agent, so the village of Neah Bay today is composed of wood frame and mobile homes. Neah Bay households have conveniences and technology comparable to those off the reservation. In the 1930s the Neah Bay Light Company brought electricity to the reservation. It provided generated electricity until 1955, when the public utility installed permanent electricity. Television arrived in Neah Bay in the 1940s. Today many people have installed satellite dishes. Most households have telephones, and many have computers and Internet access. Technology has contributed to cultural changes, but it is also being used to preserve Makah culture.

A public road that connected Neah Bay to the outside was constructed in 1931. Shortly thereafter the automobile took the place of canoe travel. Today most families in Neah Bay own automobiles, and canoes are used for racing, traveling to intertribal gatherings at other Indian villages, and whaling.

Heritage Programs

In 1932 a public school was built on ten acres donated by a Makah man named Luke Markishtum, Sr. The school was a relief to many parents, because children were often required to attend boarding schools far from home where they were forbidden to practice their tribal ways. Although the local school system did not promote Makah culture, children now could remain with their families and learn their culture at home. Incorporating Makah cultural classes in the school system would take place some thirty years later.

In the late 1960s the school system began to include basket weaving, Makah language, carving instruction, and storytelling in the curriculum. Today cultural classes in the arts and Makah language have been mainstreamed into the curriculum for both elementary and high school students with the help of the Johnson-O'Malley Act and Title 9 federal funding programs for Indian education. The Makah Cultural and Research Center staff teaches the Makah language and cultural arts.

Many students who have graduated from Neah Bay High School have gone on to college. More than one hundred Makah have earned degrees from technical schools, universities, and colleges. College extension programs through Northwest Indian College, Evergreen College, and Peninsula College are now available on the reservation. A number of people have received maritime captain licenses and own and operate large fishing vessels.

Tribal members are often trained to carry on professions that their tribal ancestors valued. Fishermen fish the ocean, the strait, and the rivers for their quota of king, silver, humpback, and sockeye salmon. Halibut and other varieties of fish are also caught, and fishermen generously share their catch with the community. Tribal artists produce and sell exceptional baskets, carvings, silver jewelry, and beadwork. A number of families travel throughout the world performing traditional dances. Seafood gatherers, seal and fish smokers, and seal and whale blubber renderers, as well as land animal hunters, provide valuable resources to the community. These people help to ensure the continuation of Makah culture for future generations.

Traditional potlatches (also known as parties) are prominent social events in Neah Bay. There are marriage, naming, memorial, anniversary, appreciation, and birthday potlatches. Inherited songs and dances, elaborate ceremonies, and extensive gift giving are customary. A potlatch can last up to two days, with as many as a thousand people in attendance. In addition to potlatches, cultural activities, work, and school fill the days in this small remote village.

Every year since 1926 on the weekend closest to August 26, the Makah Tribe celebrates Makah Days, which commemorates their becoming U.S. citizens (Indian Citizenship Act of 1924; 43 U.S. Stat. 253). During the weekend festivities the Makah community celebrates American citizenship and the survival of Makah culture. This event brings families together, rekindles friendships, and creates memories for young and old alike.

The current tribal government was informally set in motion during the 1880s when Indian agents encouraged the Makah to form their own government. In the late 1880s Neah Bay residents established a council, a police force, and a tribal court. In 1903 a town council was established. During this era, a constitution was written and implemented. Neah Bay was divided into five districts, each with an elected representative. This mimicked the democratic system wherein elected officials govern the people; however, the agency superintendent still supervised tribal activities. The town council was in effect until 1933. It groomed tribal members for the 1936 adoption of a constitution and bylaws, which promoted tribal autonomy as a result of the Howard-Wheeler, or Indian Reorganization, Act of 1934 (Williams and Helin 1984).

The governing body of the tribe consists of five Makah individuals who are elected to a three-year term. They work on a government-to-government level with federal, state, and county governments, and are decision and policy makers who oversee the direction of the Makah Tribe. Like other governing bodies, they are responsible for the health and welfare of the people they serve. Tribal offices and programs employ approximately two hundred individuals, most of whom are Makah tribal members.

A main goal of the tribe is to protect treaty rights, as these rights are continuously being challenged. The Makah tribe officially designated October 23 as the annual observance of Makah treaty rights. The Makah tribe has once again begun to exercise their whale hunting treaty right of 1855 for cultural

Eldest Tribal member, Isabel Ides (1899–2001), enjoying her 1999 Makah Day Senior Queenship. One of the tribe's beloved elders and a cultural mentor, Isabel was a fluent Makah speaker. She worked to preserve the language, was an honored basket weaver, traditional food expert, renowned storyteller, and cultural expert. Photo by Theresa Parker, Makah Cultural and Research Center.

purposes. The last whale hunt had been in 1921, at which point the Makah people made the decision to discontinue whale hunting because the gray whale had become endangered as a result of unmanaged hunting.

The gray whale is divided into two stocks, the western North Pacific and the eastern Pacific. The eastern Pacific stock migrates along the Washington coast (Gearin and DeMaster 1996). It was removed from the endangered species list in 1994, and in 1995 the tribe announced its intention to resume traditional subsistence whaling practices.

There are several reasons for this: to reestablish whaling traditions that physically, spiritually, and emotionally challenge the young people and to preserve the Makah's tribal identity as traditional whalers. Of equal importance was the need to provide interested tribal people with traditional food. The U.S. government honored the 1855 treaty and took the Makah request to the International Whaling Commission in October 1997. The Makah received a quota of twenty gray whales over a five-year period. On May 17, 1999, Makah Whalers harpooned their first whale in more than seventy years. This event received national as well as international attention.

Spoken and written history tells that the Makah have been around for a very long time. The evidence rests in the tribe's 300- to 500- year-old Ozette village and an area above it that dates to 2,000 years ago. Nearby, Cannon Ball Island has been dated to 2,500 years ago, the Hoko site is 2,700 years old, and Waatch village dates back 4,000 years. All these places are significant, but Ozette has given us the clearest picture of Makah life and has illustrated the Makah's in-depth knowledge of their environment, knowledge gained through thousands of years of living in the area.

A catastrophic mud slide buried and preserved the ancient village of Ozette in the early 1700s. With the consent of the Makah tribe, Richard Daugherty of Washington State University excavated archaeological test pits in 1966 and 1967 at Ozette near the mud slide. In winter 1970 high tides washed artifacts from their resting places and tribal officials were alerted. In 1970 the Ozette archeological project was begun. Until excavation concluded in 1981, the Makah and Washington State University students, directed by teams of archaeologists, used pressurized ocean water to slowly remove the mud from four buried houses and the exterior midden, where household items were discarded. More than 55,000 artifacts have been excavated, cleaned, identified with Makah names, cataloged, preserved, and stored or displayed. This site is recognized as one of the richest archaeological resources in the world and has inspired a cultural renaissance for the Makah.

Artifacts from all aspects of ancient tribal life were unearthed, among them beautifully carved house boards; an elaborate carved whale saddle or dorsal fin, inlaid with seven hundred sea otter teeth; numerous styles and

Makah whalers (rear canoe nearest the whale), with the assistance of
other coastal tribes, tow a gray whale to shore on May 17, 1999. After seventy years, the Makah Tribe asserted their whale hunting right outlined in
the 1855 treaty. Shortly after this photograph was taken, some 250 people
worked together to hoist the twenty-ton gray whale onshore. Photo by
Theresa Parker, Makah Cultural and Research Center.

sizes of baskets, boxes, and bowls, clothing, cradle boards, mats, hats, looms,
and toys; fishing, sealing, and whaling equipment; ceremonial gear; and
metal tools. It is speculated that the metal came from shipwrecks or trade
networks. Ancestral remains were reinterred out of respect for these people
and in keeping with cultural beliefs about death.

The Makah Tribe decided to build a museum to exhibit these cultural
items and to oversee cultural preservation programs. A team of Makah
people and Jean Jaque Andre, a professional from the British Columbia
Provincial Museum (now known as the Royal British Columbia Museum),
designed exceptional exhibit galleries to display several hundred Ozette artifacts. Andre and the Makah team, through consultation with elders, created
an interior exhibit that reflects the seasons, starting with spring whale and
seal hunting. The artifacts, illustrations, and photographs, along with realistic beach, ocean, and sea lion dioramas, accurately portray an image of
Makah life in the precontact period. The beautifully designed Makah
Cultural and Research Center (MCRC) was dedicated in 1979. In 1993 the
MCRC opened a new storage facility to house the extensive archaeological

collection. A classroom for Makah cultural classes was also added in the main building that year. In 1996 an outdoor longhouse was built that is used for salmon bakes, bone games, cultural classes, weddings, and other events. At present, an ethnobotanical garden and trail are being developed. The MCRC serves as a resource center with an extensive archive and educational and language programs.

Researchers and community members can access nonsensitive material from the archives department at the MCRC. The materials include a large selection of photographs, ethnographic books, dissertations, and information on specific topics. An on-line computer research room is available. Research agreements approved by the MCRC board are required.

The Makah Language Program officially started in 1978 with funding from the Department of Education. Before that time, language classes were taught in the Neah Bay public school during the 1960s and 1970s with Johnson-O'Malley funding. The Makah Language Program is now an integral part of the MCRC. Since the creation of the Makah alphabet, an adaptation of the international alphabet, in 1978, the MCRC has worked diligently to preserve the language. A Makah word list was made in the 1970s and is currently being updated and computerized to create a dictionary. Efforts to ensure that the language remains alive include classes for adults and children taught in the public school, at the local community college, and at the MCRC. Like their grandparents, tribal elders have generously shared their language and cultural knowledge. The knowledge connects and validates traditional culture for all who listen.

In 2000 the Makah Tribe entered into a formal agreement with the Department of the Interior to create the Makah Tribal Historic Preservation Office (THPO). The Makah THPO will assume most of the responsibilities of the State Historic Preservation Officer on Makah Reservation lands. The duties assumed include conducting a comprehensive reservation-wide cultural survey and maintaining an inventory of significant properties, identifying and nominating eligible historic properties to the National Register, developing a cultural preservation plan for tribal lands, and working with other local agencies and the public to provide training and technical assistance in historic preservation.

The Makah have successfully carried their culture into the twenty-first century, and they promote and encourage its continuation. There are ongoing cultural classes in the tribal organization, the school system, and the Makah museum that teach many facets of the culture. Knowledgeable people in the community unselfishly share what they know with other tribal members. The Makah continue to be compassionate, giving, and caring people who value their culture, each other, and life.

Whale being processed on a beach in Neah Bay. Several Makah tribal members are using traditional techniques to process whale meat and blubber. The skeletal remains are being reconstructed by the Neah Bay High School carpentry class for exhibition at the Makah Cultural and Research Center. Photo by Theresa Parker, Makah Cultural and Research Center.

Visitor Opportunities

Many visitors come to see the Makah Cultural and Research Center, but a trip to Neah Bay should include the Cape Flattery Trail, a three-quarter-mile cedar plank boardwalk leading to the northwestern tip of the United States. Cedar, hemlock, spruce, and alder trees invite contemplation and the Pacific Ocean beckons. The tribe welcomes visitors to all of the following sites:

- Makah Cultural and Research Center Museum and Craft Shop. Summer hours 10:00 A.M. to 5:00 P.M.; winter hours Wednesday through Sunday 10:00 A.M. TO 5:00 P.M.
- Locally owned tribal art, T-shirt, and gift shops.
- Cape Flattery Trail. Open year-round.
- Ocean and Fuca Strait Beaches. Open year-round. No seafood or shell gathering is permitted on tribal beaches.
- Makah Marina. A year-round protected boat haven with a tribal/marine sanctuary information center.
- Charter boats for bottom and salmon fishing, sight-seeing, and diving.

- The Makah Days celebration is held the third weekend in August. This celebration commemorates the 1924 decision to include Indians as American citizens. The first Makah day was held in August 1926. Tribal songs and dances, canoe races, field races, salmon bake, talent show/ queen coronation, and sidewalk booths provide lots of fun and interesting entertainment. The public is always welcome!
- Makah Fourth of July Fireworks. The best on the peninsula!

NOTES

1. This is the Makah word for themselves. *Makah* is a Coast Salish word used during treaty times.

SUGGESTED READING

Densmore, Frances. 1939. *Nootka and Quileute Music.* Bureau of American Ethnology. Bulletin 110. Washington, D.C.

A Gift from the Past: Indian America. 1994. Video. Narrated by Wes Studi.

Marr, Carol, with photographs by Samuel G. Morse. 1987. *Portrait in Time.* Seattle: Makah Cultural and Research Center in cooperation with the Washington State Historical Society.

Afterword: Salmonberry Memories

The experience of writing this book over the past three years has brought us profound rewards in the respect we feel for one another and the achievement we share. And what better way to conclude this project than to celebrate the emergence of the bright reddish purple salmonberry blooms of spring. However different each winter day might be—whether it is snowing, blowing, sunny and icy cold, or raining, raining, raining—there is nothing more joyous than seeing the glowing flowers emerge from the barren branches of winter and the anticipation of the succulent sprouts and fruit. What follows are the memories that the first sign of spring, the salmonberry, sparked in the authors of this book.

> Salmonberries are the first sign of spring. The hummingbirds come out and then you know a new season has begun. (Jamie Valadez, Elwha Klallam)

> When the salmonberry bloom the blueback salmon runs return to the Quinault River. (Justine James, Quinault)

> We were taught to carefully look inside the berry, just in case there might be a baby slug inside! If there wasn't a baby slug, we would take the berries home, wash them, and then eat the tasty morsels. (Vi Riebe, Hoh)

> The salmonberry grows in the most beautiful places, under the shade of the licorice ferns, which grow on the tall trees. It's like a magical path taking me to memories and sweet tastes. (Bonnie [James] Graft, Skokomish)

> Salmonberries make me think back to when I was a young girl and would pick the berries to eat with my breakfast. It seems like it was always sunny back then. I now take my son and nieces and nephews berry picking. (Marie Hebert, Port Gamble S'Klallam)

> Warm and wonderful days! From the age of one, I was lucky to be spending every day with my father, Charlie Fitzgerald, either in the hay fields or logging in the woods. When logging, salmon berries were one of my favorite snacks and being able to get a drink of water out of a stream flowing down from the mountains. My dad would pick the berries and cup them in his hand for me to eat and would dip the same cupped hands to hold water until I was old enough to drink by myself without falling into the creek. (Kathy Duncan, Jamestown S'Klallam)

When I was a young girl I visited my grandmother on the reservation in the summer. I only lived ten miles away, but the attitude toward berries was much different in town: they were weeds. On the reservation salmonberries were treasured not only for the taste, but for the lesson to take the time to stop and pick them off the bush. At that moment eating the delicious berries was the most important task. I learned to take time to enjoy what nature had to offer in the natural setting. No plastic wrapping or cardboard box. It is a lesson that has given me many precious memories of berry picking excursions with my children. (Genny Rogers, Skokomish)

I used to take my four children on nature walks to our salmonberry patch. The kids would race to get the big juicy reddish berries hanging on burdened limbs. Sometimes they would remember old Aunt Helen and they would pick the best salmonberries for her. Helen's eyes sparkled with delight as she accepted her bowl of delicious salmonberries. (Melissa Peterson, Makah)

When I think of salmonberries, I think of wading in Little Skookum Creek with my cousin when I was nine years old. The berries would be thickest and biggest where they were hanging over the shady creek. It was so calm and cool. (Andi VanderWal, Squaxin Island)

Just some of Mother Nature's treats, salmonberries ever so sweet.
The crawlies and birds eat them too. They scatter the seeds for me and you
For next season's sun and rains repeat.

Soft green sprouts in May
Just peel the skins away.
Another morsel not well known
With bright green flesh when not full grown. Then vernalized before the
    summer ray.

A handful of youthful leaves of green,
When steeped is somewhere in between
The rainbow and the smell of spring.
A surprise the salmonberries' leaves can bring. There's a plethora for you
    to glean. (Chris Morganroth III, Quileute)

Every season has special meaning, memories, and smells: salmon spawning in the rivers, plants to be picked as soon as they sprout, activities to enjoy with the young. This is our common thread. We have a legacy to hand down to future generations, our history, our memories, and our strength. In this book we hope we have conveyed a better understanding of who we are.

Bibliography

Adams, George N. 1951. Address to the National Congress of American Indians. Family collection.

Adams, Harriette (Jamestown S'Klallam). 1988. Tribal Interview, April 15. Jamestown S'Klallam Archives.

Amoss, Pamela T. 1990. "The Indian Shaker Church." Pp. 633–39 in *Handbook of North American Indians*, vol. 7: *Northwest Coast*, edited by Wayne Suttles. Washington, D.C.: Smithsonian Institution Press.

Andrade, Manuel J. 1931. *Quileute Texts.* New York: Columbia University Press.

Andrews, Ralph W. 1956. *Indian Primitive.* Bonanza Books. New York: Crown Publishers.

ARCIA (Annual Reports of the Commissioner of Indian Affairs) 1857, 1860, 1862, 1872. Washington, D.C.: Government Printing Office.

Asher, Brad. 1999. *Beyond the Reservation: Indians, Settlers, and the Law in Washington Territory, 1853–1889.* Norman: University of Oklahoma Press.

Atwater, Brian F., Marco Cisternas V., Joanne Bourgeois, Walter C. Dudley, James W. Hendley II, and Peter H. Stauffer. 1999. *Surviving a Tsunami: Lessons From Chile, Hawaii, and Japan.* U.S. Geological Survey Circular 1187. Washington, D.C.: Government Printing Office.

Atwater, B. F., and A. L. Moore. 1992. "A Tsunami 1000 Years Ago in Puget Sound, Washington." *Science* 258:1614–17.

Barnett, Homer G. 1957. *Indian Shakers: A Messianic Cult of the Pacific Northwest.* Carbondale: Southern Illinois University Press.

Bennett, Walter (Elwha Klallam). 1992. Tribal Interview, September 1. Quinault Archives.

Bergland, Eric O. 1983. "Olympic National Park Archeological Basemap Study: Summary Report to Superintendent Chandler." Report on File, U.S. Department of the Interior, National Park Service, Pacific Northwest Region, Seattle, Wash.

Bergland, Eric, and Jerry Marr. 1988. *Prehistoric Life on the Olympic Peninsula: The First Inhabitants of a Great American Wilderness.* Seattle, Wash.: Pacific Northwest National Parks and Forests Association.

Bestor, Frank H. 1971. "Are You Listening Neighbor? . . . ." Olympia, Wash.: Office of the Indian Affairs Task Force, Governors Office.

BIA (Bureau of Indian Affairs). 1838–63. Documents Relating to the Negotiation of Ratified and Unratified Treaties with Various Indian Tribes, 1801–1869. Manuscripts, microfilm T494, rolls 4,5,8 Record Group 75. National Archives, Washington, D.C.

———. 1980. "Recommendation and Summary of Evidence for Proposed Finding for Federal Acknowledgement of the Jamestown Band of Clallam Indians of Washington Pursuant to 25 CFR 54." Tribal Government Series.

Bishop, Thomas. 1915. "An Appeal to the Government to Fulfill Sacred Promises Made 61 Years Ago." December 24. Report of Gerald Member of Board of Management to President of the United States, June 15, 1914.

Bremerton Sun. 1957. Armed Forces Edition. May 17:3.

Brown, Bruce. 1990. *Mountain in the Clouds: A Search for the Wild Salmon.* New York: Collier Books.

Chinook Northwest and Martino and Associates. 1998. "Estimated Economic Damage to the Skokomish Indian Tribe from Unregulated Construction and Operation of the City of Tacoma's Cushman Hydroelectric Project, 1926–1997." Report prepared for the Skokomish Indian Tribe, September.

Clinton, William Jefferson. 1998. "Remarks by the President to White House Conference Building Economic Self-Determination in Indian Communities." Washington, D.C.: Office of the Press Secretary, August 6.

Cole, S. C., B. F. Atwater, P. T. McCutcheon, J. K. Stein, and E. Hemphill-Haley. 1996. "Earthquake-induced Burial of Archaeological Sites along the Southern Washington Coast about A.D. 1700." *Geoarcheology* 11: 165–77.

Coman, Edwin T., Jr., and Helen M. Gibbs. 1949. *Time, Tide and Timber.* Stanford: Stanford University Press.

Conca, Dave, and Kirstie Haertel. 1995. "Systemwide Archeological Inventory Program (SAIP) Interim Report, Fiscal Year 1994." Cultural Resource Files, Olympic National Park.

Curtis, Edward S. 1913. The North American Indian. Vol. 9. New York: Johnson Reprint Corporation.

Daugherty, Richard D. 1948-49. NB1-4. Unpub. ethnographic notebooks on the Hoh.

Deloria, Vine, Jr. 1983. *American Indians, American Justice.* Austin: University of Texas Press.

Duwamish et al. v. U.S.A. 1927. U.S. Court of Claims, No. F–275.

Eells, Myron. [1886]1972. *Ten Years of Missionary Work among the Indians at Skokomish, Washington Territory.* Seattle, Wash.: The Shorey Book Store.

———[1887]1971. "Decrease of Population among the Indians of Puget Sound." *American Antiquarian and Oriental Journal* 95(5): 271–76.

———1892. "Aboriginal Geographic Names in the State of Washington." *American Anthropologist.* 5: 27–35.

Elmendorf, William W. [1960] 1992. The Structure of Twana Culture. Pullman: Washington State University Press.

———1961a. "Skokomish and Other Coast Salish Tales." *Washington State University Research Studies* 29(1): 1–37.

———1961b. "Skokomish and Other Coast Salish Tales." *Washington State University Research Studies.* 29(3): 119–50.

Farrand, Livingston. 1902. "Traditions of the Quinault Indians." Publications of Jesup North Pacific Expedition. *Memoirs of the American Museum of Natural History* 4(3): 77–132.

Frachtenberg, Leo. 1916. Unpublished ethnographic notebooks on the Quileute and Hoh in the American Philosophical Society Library, Philadelphia.

Gearin, Patrick J., and Douglas DeMaster. 1996. *Gray Whales in Washington State.* Seattle: National Marine Mammal Laboratory.

Gibbs, George. [1855]1877. "Tribes of Western Washington and Northwestern Oregon." Edited by John Wesley Powell. *Contributions to North American Ethnology* 1(2): 157–361. Washington, D.C.: U.S. Geographical and Geological Survey of the Rocky Mountain Region. Reprint Seattle, Wash.: Shorey Book Store. 1970.

Gunther, Erna. 1924. Field notebooks. Accession No. 614-70-20. Manuscripts and University Archives Division, University of Washington.

———1925. "Klallam Folk Tales." *University of Washington Publications in Anthropology* 1(4): 113–69.

———1927. "Klallam Ethnography." *University of Washington Publications in Anthropology* 1(5): 171–314.

———1949. "The Shaker Religion of the Northwest." Pp. 37–76 *Indians of the Urban Northwest*, edited by Marian W. Smith. New York: Columbia University Press.

Gustafson, Carl E., Delbert W. Gilbow, and Richard D. Daugherty. 1979. "The Manis Mastodon Site: Early Man on the Olympic Peninsula." *Canadian Journal of Archaeology* 3: 157–164.

Hagan, William T. 1988. "United States Indian Policies, 1860-1900." Pp. 51–65 in *Handbook of North American Indians*, vol. 4: *History of Indian-White Relations*, edited by Wilcomb E. Washburn, Washington, D.C.: Smithsonian Institution Press.

Harmon, Alexandra. 1998. *Indians in the Making: Ethnic Relations and Indian Identities around Puget Sound*. Berkeley: University of California Press.

Harrington, John P. 1942. Alsea, Siuslaw, Coos: Vocabularies, Linguistic Notes, Ethnographic and Historical Notes. Microfilm, reel nos. 021–024. John Peabody Harrington Papers, Alaska/Northwest Coast. National Archaeological Archives, Washington, D.C.

Hess, Thomas. 1976. *A Dictionary of Puget Salish*. Seattle: University of Washington Press.

Heusser, Calvin J. 1973. "Environmental Sequence Following the Fraser Advance of the Juan de Fuca Lobe, Washington." *Quaternary Research* (3): 284–306.

Hodge, Frederick W., ed. 1907–10. *Handbook of North American Indians North of Mexico*. 2 vols. Bureau of American Ethnology Bulletin 30. Washington, D.C. Reprint, New York: Rowman & Littlefield, 1979.

Holt, L. M. 1913. "Report on Proposed Dam on Skokomish River, Washington." Superintendent of Irrigation, United States Indian Service, Portland Area Office, Federal Regulatory Commission 19749, Power & Reservoir Sites. Record Group 75, Federal Archives and Records Center, Seattle, Wash.

ICC (Indian Claims Commission). 1979. "Clallam Claims Judgement Distribution Master Plan, Clallam Judgement Funds." Indian Claims Commission Docket 134.

Ives, Danette "Danno." 1997. Interview, June. Port Gamble S'Klallam Archives.

Jamestown S'Klallam Tribe. 1998. *Annual Report*. Jamestown S'Klallam Tribe.

Johnson, Harris "Brick" (Jamestown S'Klallam). 1988. Tribal Interview, March 13. Jamestown S'Klallam Archives.

Krise, Mary Bobb. 1940. "The Origin of the Shaker Church." Interview, January 27. Mason County Pioneer and Historical Society, Shelton, Wash.

Lambert, Mary Ann. 1992. "Point No Point Treaty." Pp. 66–68 in *Shadows of Our Ancestors*, edited by Jerry Gorsline. Port Townsend, Wash.: Empty Bowl Press.

Lane, Barbara. 1973. "Makah Economy circa 1855 and the Makah Treaty: A Cultural Analysis." In *Political and Economic Aspects of Indian-White Culture Contact in Western Washington in the Mid-Nineteenth Century*. (Prepared for *U.S. v. Washington*).

————1977. "Identity, Treaty Status and Fisheries of the Port Gamble Indian Community, July 25, 1977." Prepared for the U.S. Department of the Interior and the Port Gamble Indian Community.

Lane, Robert Brockstedt, and Barbara Lane. 1977. "Treaties of the Puget Sound: 1854–1855." Prepared for Institute for the Development of Indian Law, Washington, D.C.

Langness, L. L. 1984. "Individual Psychology and Cultural Change: An Ethnohistorical Case from the Klallam." Pp. 255–80 in *The Tsimshian and Their Neighbors of the North Pacific Coast*, edited by Jay Miller and Carol M. Eastman. Seattle: University of Washington Press.

Marine Mammal Protection Act. 1995. *Marine Mammal Protection Act of 1972 as Amended*. Washington D.C. Marine Mammal Commission. February.

Matson, R. G., and Gary Coupland. 1995. *The Prehistory of the Northwest Coast*. San Diego: Academic Press.

Meany, Edmond S. 1905. "Twana and Clallam Indians. Aborigines of Hood Canal." *Seattle Post-Intelligencer*, October 22.

————1920. "Indians of the Olympic Penninsula." *The Mountaineer* 13(1): 34–39.

————[1907]1942. *Vancouver's Discovery of Puget Sound*. Portland, Ore.: Binfords and Mort.

Meriam, Lewis. 1928. *The Problem of Indian Administration*. Baltimore: Johns Hopkins University Press. Reprint, New York: Johnson Reprint Corporation, 1971.

Meyers, Edward C. 1994. *Children of the Thunderbird: Legends and Myths from the West Coast*. Blaine, Wash: Hancock House.

Minor, R., and W. C. Grant. 1996. "Earthquake-induced Subsidence and Burial of Late Holocene Archaeological Sites, Northern Oregon Coast." *American Antiquities* 61: 772–81.

Montler, Timothy. 1995. *Learning Klallam: Materials for Learning and Teaching the Klallam Language*. Port Angeles, Wash.: Elwha Klallam Language Program.

Moore v. U.S. 1946. Milo Moore, Director of Fisheries of the State of Washington, and Don W. Clarke, Director of Game of the State of Washington, Appellants, v. United States of America, Appellee. Brief for the Quillehute Tribe of Indians. Kenneth R. L. Simmons, Attorney. Billings, Montana, July.

Morgan, Vera. 1998. Letter to Kathy Duncan, Jamestown S'Klallam Tribe. August 14.

Morgenroth, Chris. 1991. *Footprints in the Olympics: An Autobiography*. Edited by Katherine M. Flaherty. Fairfield, Wash: Ye Galleon Press.

Morrison, Homer L. 1939. "A Clallam Community: A Study of the Rehabilitation Program of the Clallam Indians in the Valley of the Lower Elwha in Clallam

County, Washington." Superintendent, Indian Education. June 6. University of
Washington, Special Collections.

NWIFC (Northwest Indian Fisheries Commission News). 1999–2000. "Federal
Government Buys Elwha Dams." 14 no.4 (Winter):4.

Office of Inspector General. 1995. *Jamestown Audit Report*. Jamestown S'Klallam
Tribe, Blyn, Wash.

Olson, Ronald. 1936. *The Quinault Indians*. Seattle: University of Washington Press.

Olympic National Park. 1998. "Elwha River Running an Obstacle Course from
Mountains to Sea." Olympic National Park Brochure.

Owens, Kenneth N., and Alton S. Donnelly. 1985 The Wreck of the "*Sv. Nikolai*."
Portland, Ore.: Western Imprints.

Patterson, Harold. 1968. "The Myth and the Modern Curriculum." Unpublished
manuscript.

————1967. "CAP—A Community Action Progress Report." Quinault Indian
Nation, Environmental Protection Division.

Peninsula Daily News. 1998. "Babbitt Says Elwha Dams Safe for Now." July 20.

Pettitt, George A. 1950. "The Quileute of La Push: 1775–1945." *Anthropological
Records* 14:1.

Pevar, Stephen L. 1992. *The Rights of Indians and Tribes: The Basic ACLU Guide to
Indian and Tribal Rights*. Carbondale: Southern Illinois University Press.

Port Gamble S'Klallam Tribe. 1971–75. Klallam History from Manuscript and
Memory. Port Gamble S'Klallam Archives.

————1994. "Pride Is Our Heritage." March. Newsletter.

Powell, Jay V. 1968–2001. Field notes. In possession of Powell.

Powell, Jay, *et al.* 1995. Sol Duc Pilot Watershed Analysis (Tribal Cultural Module).
October 30. U.S. Forest Service, Olympic National Forest, Wash.

Reagan, Albert B. 1934a. "Plants Used by the Hoh and Quileute Indians."
Transactions of the Kansas Academy of Science 37: 55–70.

————1934b. "Some Traditions of the West Coast Indians." *Utah Academy of
Sciences Arts and Letters* 11: 73–93.

Reagan, Albert B., and L. V. W. Walters. 1933. "Tales from the Hoh and Quileute."
Journal of American Folklore 46: 297–346.

Reis, Mark. 1987. "Indian Land Tenure and Economic Development Project: Phase
I." Northwest Renewable Resources Center, Seattle, Wash.

Roblin, Charles E. 1919. Correspondence from Special Indian Agent, Charles
Roblin to Commissioner of Indian Affairs. January 31, 1919. M-1434, Roll 1.
National Archives, Seattle, Wash.

Satake, K., K. Shimazaki, Y. Tsuji, and K. Ueda. 1996. "Time and Size of a Giant
Earthquake in Cascadia Inferred from Japanese Tsunami Record of January
1700." *Nature* 379: 246–49.

Schalk, Randall. 1988. "The Evolution and Diversification of Native Land Use
Systems on the Olympic Peninsula: A Research Design." National Park Service.

Scovill, Douglas. 1987. "Conservation of Ethnographic Resources: A New and
Developing Program in the National Park Service." *Trends: Park Practice
Program* 24(4).

Seattle Post Intelligencer. 1947. "Plenty Smart Those Paleface Bostons, but Why Steal Body: Last of Clallams Cling to Site of Ancestors." August 26.

Seattle Times. 1961. "School's Needed, Says Oldest Quinault." April 18.

Simmons, Michael (Indian Agent, WT). 1859. Letter to R. Geary (Superintendent of Indian Affairs, Washington and Oregon) July 1, 1859. Attachment No. 180. Annual Report Secretary of Interior 1859: 760–66. Executive Documents printed by U.S. Senate, 36th Cong., 1st sess., 1859–60. CIS U.S. Serial 1023, Microforms, University of Washington Libraries.

———1860. Letter to R. Geary (Superintendent of Indian Affairs, Washington and Oregon) July 1, 1860. Attachment No. 78. Annual Report Secretary of Interior 1860: 410–22. Executive Documents printed by U.S. Senate, 36th Cong., 2d sess., 1860–61. CIS U.S. Serial 1078, Microforms, University of Washington Libraries.

Singh, Ram Raj Prasad. 1966. "Aboriginal Economic System of the Olympic Peninsula Indians, Western Washington." *Anthropological Society Papers* 4.

Skokomish Tribe. 1991. *Portrait of a Tribe: An Introduction to the Skokomish Indian Tribe.* Shelton, Wash.: Skokomish Indian Tribe.

———"Restore the Skokomish River." Newsletter. March.

Smith, Leroy. 1976. *Pioneers of the Olympic Peninsula.* Forks, Wash.: Olympic Graphic Arts.

Sotomish, Clinton (Quinault). 1994. Interview, September. Quinault Archives.

Stevens, Isaac. 1855. *Narrative and Final Report of Explorations for a Route for a Pacific Railroad Near the Forty-seventh and Forty-ninth Parallels of North Latitude from St. Paul to Puget Sound.* Geographical Memoir. 8.

Storm, Jacqueline M., David Chance, Jim Harp, Karen Harp, Lawrence Lestelle, Sarah Colleen Sotomish, and Larry Workman. 1990. *Land of the Quinault.* Taholah, Wash: Quinault Indian Nation.

Swindell, Edward G., Jr. 1942. "Report on the Source, Nature and Extent of the Fishing, Hunting and Miscellaneous related Rights of Certian [*sic*] Indian Tribes in Washington and Oregon Together with Affidavits Showing Locations of a Number of Usual and Accustomed Fishing Grounds and Stations." Testimony by members of the Quileute Indian Tribe for the U.S. Indian Service, July. Cultural Resource File, Olympic National Park.

Szasz, Margaret Connell, and Carmelita S. Ryan. 1988. "American Indian Education." Pp. 284–300 in *Handbook of North American Indians*, vol. 4: *History of Indian-White Relations*, edited by Wilcomb E. Washburn. Washington, D.C.: Smithsonian Institution Press.

Taylor, Herbert C., Jr. 1963. "Aboriginal Populations of the Lower Northwest Coast." *Pacific Northwest Quarterly* 54(4): 158–65.

Thompson, Laurence C., and M. Dale Kinkade. 1990. "Languages." Pp.30–51 in *Handbook of North American Indians*, vol. 7: *Northwest Coast*, edited by Wayne Suttles. Washington, D.C.: Smithsonian Institution Press.

Thompson, Nile. 1979. *Twana Dictionary (Student Version).* Twana Language Project. Shelton, Wash.: Skokomish Indian Tribe.

Ullman, Bud, Barbara Lane, and Hazel Smith. 1977. *Handbook on Legislation and Litigation Affecting the Quinault Reservation.* Taholah, Wash.: Quinault Indian Nation.

U.S. Department of the Interior. 1995. *Final Environmental Impact Statement: Elwha River Ecosystem Restoration, Olympic National Park, Washington.* June.

U.S. Government. 1994. Memorandum for the Heads of Executive Departments and Agencies. Subject: Government-to-Government Relations with Native American Tribal Governments. April 29.

Wagner, Henry. 1933. *Spanish Explorations in the Strait of Juan de Fuca.* Santa Ana, Calif.: Fine Arts Press.

Wagner, Henry R., and A. J. Baker, eds. and trans. 1930. "Fray Benito de la Sierra's Account of the Hezeta Expedition to the Northwest Coast in 1775." *California Historical Quarterly* 9(3): 201–42.

Waterman, T. T. 1920. Puget Sound Geography. MS No. 1864. National Anthropological Archives, Smithsonian Institution, Washington, D.C.

Wells, Richard. 1997. "An Overview of the Comprehensive Land Development Use Plan for the Quinault Indian Reservation." Department of Community Development. February.

Whitebrook, Robert Ballard. 1959. *Coastal Exploration of Washington.* Palo Alto, Calif.: Pacific Books.

Whitener, Wesley, and Florence Sigo (Squaxin Island). 1975. Interview, Squaxin Island Archives.

Williams, Alfred. 1995. Interview, June 7. Quinault Archives.

Williams, Theresa, and William Helin. 1984. *Makah Forest Management Plan.* Neah Bay, Wash.: Makah Tribal Council.

Willoughby, C. 1889. "Indians of the Quinaielt Agency, Washington Territory." Pp. 267–82 in *Annual Report of the Smithsonian Institution for the Year 1886.* Washington, D.C.

Wood, Robert L. 1989. *Across the Olympic Mountains: The Press Expedition, 1889–90.* Seattle: Mountaineers and University of Washington Press.

Yakima Herald. 1937. March 7.

Yamaguchi, David K., Brian F. Atwater, Daniel E. Bunker, Boyd E. Benson, and Marion S. Reid. 1997. "Tree-Ring Dating the 1700 Cascadia Earthquake." *Nature* 389: 922–23.

Index

Adams, George, 72
Alders, 155, 166
Aldwell, Thomas, 28
Allotments, reservation-land, 109–10
Alphabet: Klallam, 31; Makah, 165
Amanda Park (Quinault Res. community), 111
American Indian Religious Freedom Act, 14–15, 72
American Missionary Association, 71–72
Andre, Jean Jaque, 164
Annual cycle, Quileute, 146
Arrows. See Bow and arrow
Artifacts, 6–8, 62, 79, 96, 163–64
Artwork, 46, 78, 85, 96, 148
Assembly of God (denom.), 143
Astor, John Jacob, 10
Astoria, Wash., 10

Bahaada (Makah village), 152, 159
Balch, James, 36, 42
Bark: medicinal, 154; working of tree, 143, 155
Barnacles, edible, 122, 154
Basketry, 45, 69–71, 80, 85, 88, 96, 114, 121, 132, 143, 147, 155, 161; as Makah Res. school subject, 160
Baskets, as artifacts, 6, 164
Beach grass, 114
Beadwork, 45, 161
Bear, 66, 123, 126, 140, 154; in Hoh legend, 119; in Squaxin Island tradition, 86, 92
Bear grass, 114
Beaver, 68, 140, 154; in Quileute tradition, 138, 139; in Squaxin Island belief, 86, 92
Beecher Bay (Klallam village), 23
Berries, 7, 11, 66–68, 71, 85, 86, 88, 100, 106, 138, 142, 143,154. See also Salmonberries; Thimbleberries
BIA. See Bureau of Indian Affairs
Bison, 7
Blankets, Squaxin Island, 85
Blubber, sea-mammal, 154, 161
Blue jay, in Quileute tradition, 139
Bobcat, 123
Bodega y Quadra, Juan Francisco de la, 10, 108
Bones, as tools, 154
Boston Charlie (Klallam medicine man), 23
Bottomfish, 153, 154
Bow and arrow, Quileute mastery of, 140
Brake ferns, 142

British, to Olympic Peninsula, 5, 10, 129
Buildings, cedar, 155. See also Longhouses
Bulbs, edible, 154
Bureau of Indian Affairs (BIA): IRA presented by, 26; S'Klallam and, 19–20
Burke Act, 110

Calendar, Quileute, 146
California, state of: gambling in, 96
Camas, 87, 106, 137, 142, 143
Cannon Ball Island, 163
Canoes, 8, 31, 61, 78, 85, 121, 136, 143, 147, 155, 160, 167; Hoh oceangoing, 123; Quinault mastery of, 101–103; racing of, 102–103, 167; varieties of, 8, 101, 153; war, 153; whaling from, 106
Caribou, 7
Carrots, 142
Carvings, 45, 160, 161. See also Canoes
Casinos, tribal, 47, 96, 116
Catholicism, 51, 90
Cattails, 114
Cedar, 6, 8, 101, 103, 114, 136, 152, 153, 166; for canoe seats, 106; clothing made of, 143, 154, 155; as elk-hunting resource, 123; in Hoh belief, 121; Makah use of, 155; Quileute use of, 143; as Squaxin Island raw material, 83, 85, 86, 88; uses of, 155
Changer. See K'wati
Chehalis Tribe, 11, 99, 110, 129
Chemakum (lang.), 127, 137
Chemakum Tribe, 4, 11, 19, 51, 53, 54, 127; assimilation of, 69, 127; and Point No Point treaty, 68–69; in Quileute tradition, 136–37
Chemawa Indian School, 13, 26–27, 87
Cherry trees, 85; wild, 155
Chiefs: Makah, 156; Quileute, 147
Chimakuan language family, 3, 4. See also Chemakum (lang.); Quileute (lang.)
China slippers, 122
Chinook Jargon, 4, 86, 129, 157
Chinook Tribe, 11, 99, 110
Chinook winds, 136
Chitons, 142, 154
Christianity, imposed, 13. See also Assembly of God; Catholicism; Missionaries; Shaker church
Church Point, 90–91